Welcome

May all who come as guests leave as friends.

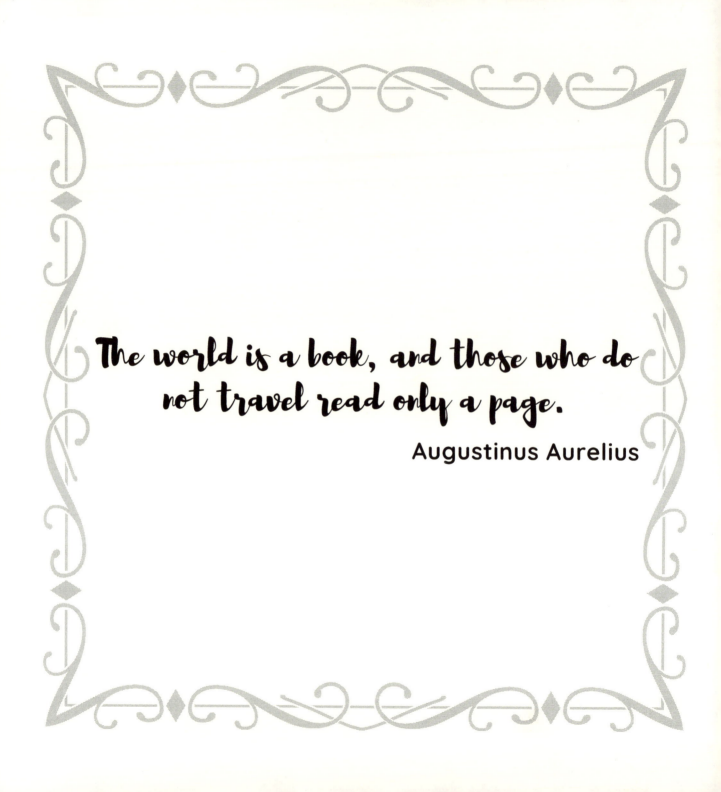

The world is a book, and those who do not travel read only a page.

Augustinus Aurelius

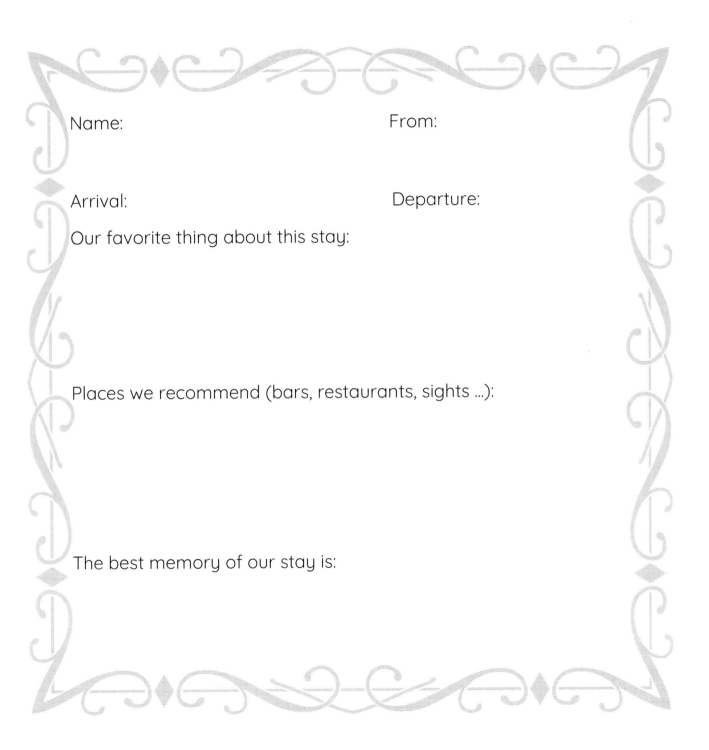

Name: From:

Arrival: Departure:

Our favorite thing about this stay:

Places we recommend (bars, restaurants, sights ...):

The best memory of our stay is:

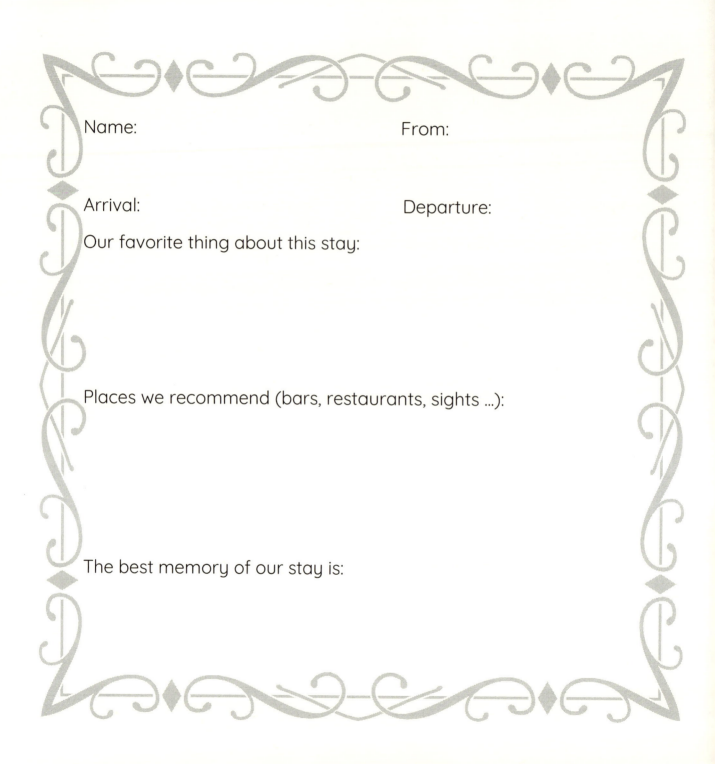

Name: From:

Arrival: Departure:

Our favorite thing about this stay:

Places we recommend (bars, restaurants, sights ...):

The best memory of our stay is:

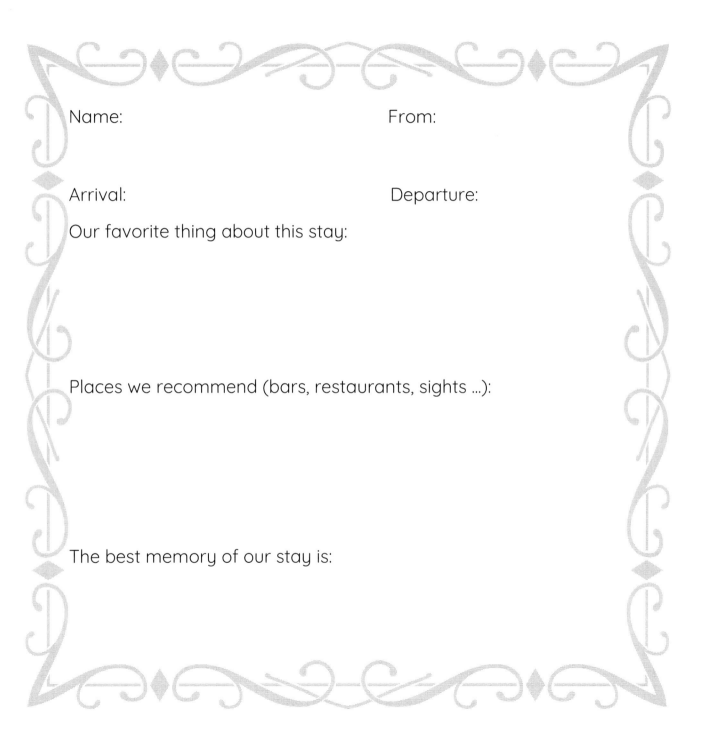

Name: From:

Arrival: Departure:

Our favorite thing about this stay:

Places we recommend (bars, restaurants, sights ...):

The best memory of our stay is:

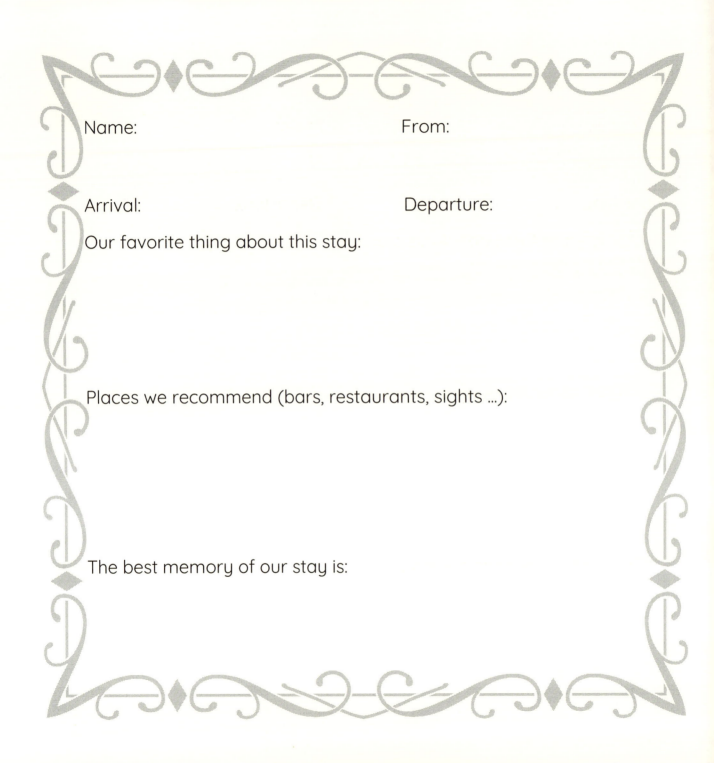

Name: From:

Arrival: Departure:

Our favorite thing about this stay:

Places we recommend (bars, restaurants, sights ...):

The best memory of our stay is:

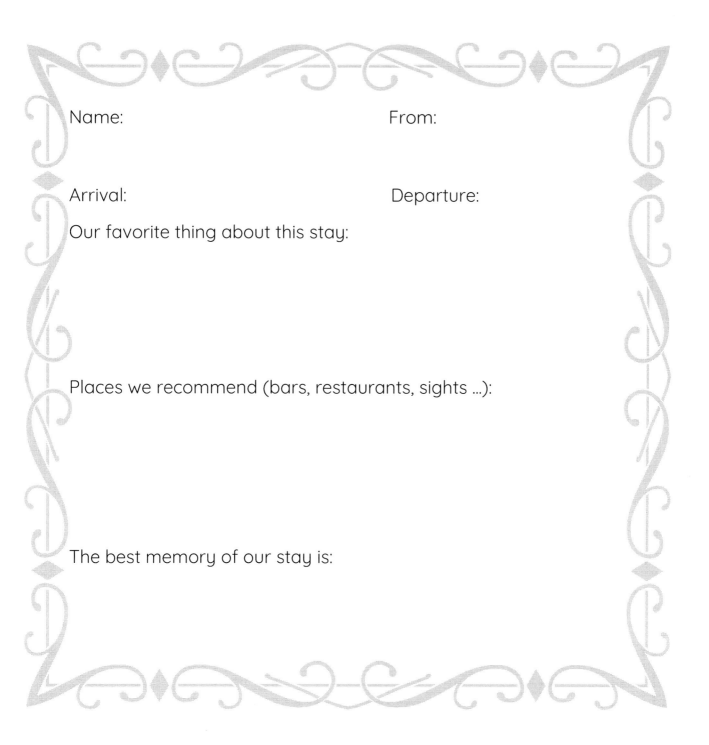

Name: From:

Arrival: Departure:

Our favorite thing about this stay:

Places we recommend (bars, restaurants, sights ...):

The best memory of our stay is:

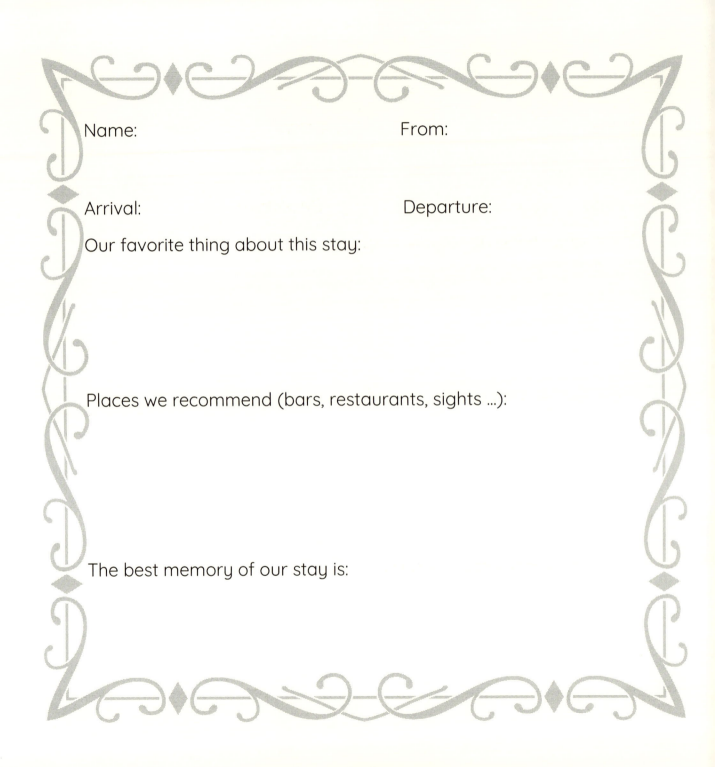

Name: From:

Arrival: Departure:

Our favorite thing about this stay:

Places we recommend (bars, restaurants, sights ...):

The best memory of our stay is:

Name: From:

Arrival: Departure:

Our favorite thing about this stay:

Places we recommend (bars, restaurants, sights ...):

The best memory of our stay is:

Name: From:

Arrival: Departure:

Our favorite thing about this stay:

Places we recommend (bars, restaurants, sights ...):

The best memory of our stay is:

Name: From:

Arrival: Departure:

Our favorite thing about this stay:

Places we recommend (bars, restaurants, sights ...):

The best memory of our stay is:

Name: From:

Arrival: Departure:

Our favorite thing about this stay:

Places we recommend (bars, restaurants, sights ...):

The best memory of our stay is:

Name: From:

Arrival: Departure:

Our favorite thing about this stay:

Places we recommend (bars, restaurants, sights ...):

The best memory of our stay is:

Name: From:

Arrival: Departure:

Our favorite thing about this stay:

Places we recommend (bars, restaurants, sights ...):

The best memory of our stay is:

Name: From:

Arrival: Departure:

Our favorite thing about this stay:

Places we recommend (bars, restaurants, sights ...):

The best memory of our stay is:

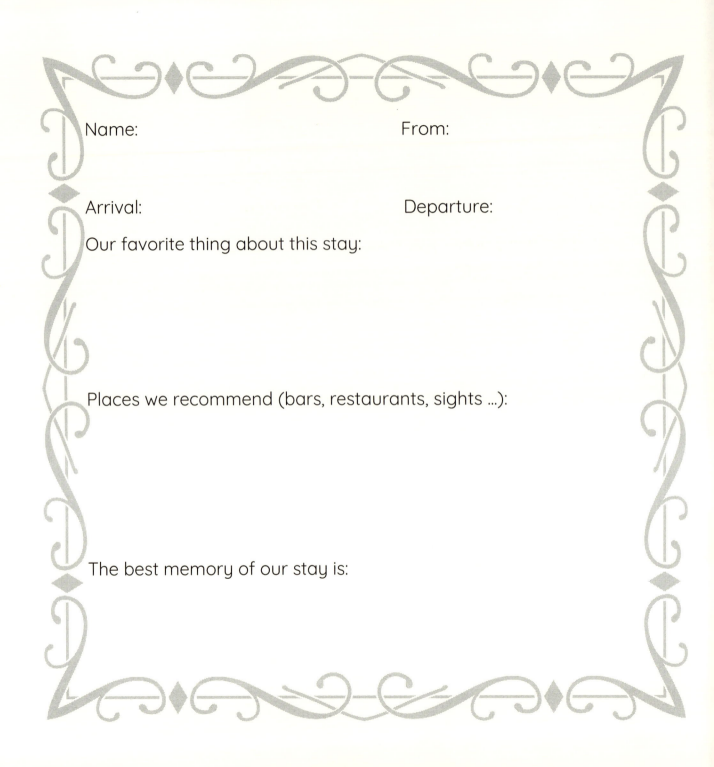

Name: From:

Arrival: Departure:

Our favorite thing about this stay:

Places we recommend (bars, restaurants, sights ...):

The best memory of our stay is:

Name: From:

Arrival: Departure:

Our favorite thing about this stay:

Places we recommend (bars, restaurants, sights ...):

The best memory of our stay is:

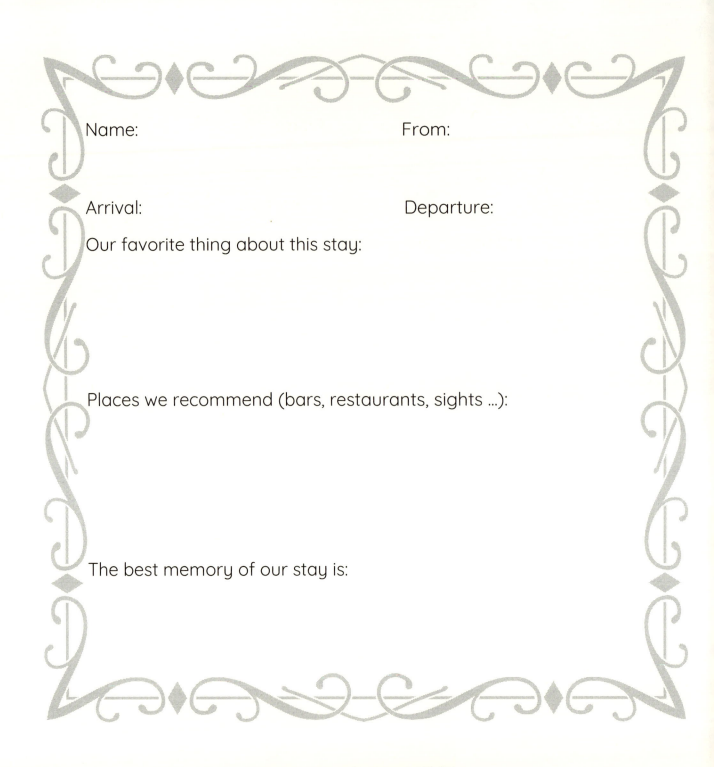

Name: From:

Arrival: Departure:

Our favorite thing about this stay:

Places we recommend (bars, restaurants, sights ...):

The best memory of our stay is:

Name: From:

Arrival: Departure:

Our favorite thing about this stay:

Places we recommend (bars, restaurants, sights ...):

The best memory of our stay is:

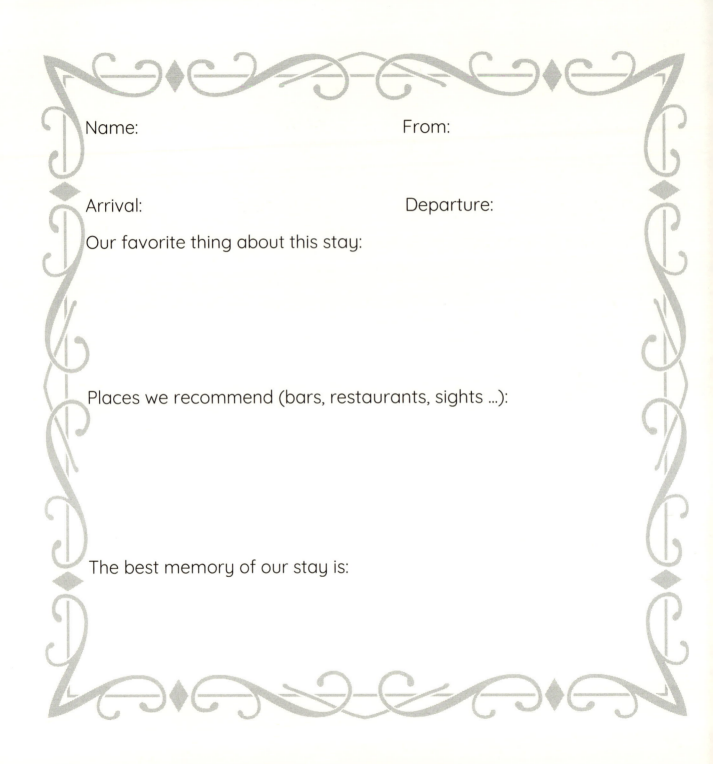

Name: From:

Arrival: Departure:

Our favorite thing about this stay:

Places we recommend (bars, restaurants, sights ...):

The best memory of our stay is:

Name: From:

Arrival: Departure:

Our favorite thing about this stay:

Places we recommend (bars, restaurants, sights ...):

The best memory of our stay is:

Name: From:

Arrival: Departure:

Our favorite thing about this stay:

Places we recommend (bars, restaurants, sights ...):

The best memory of our stay is:

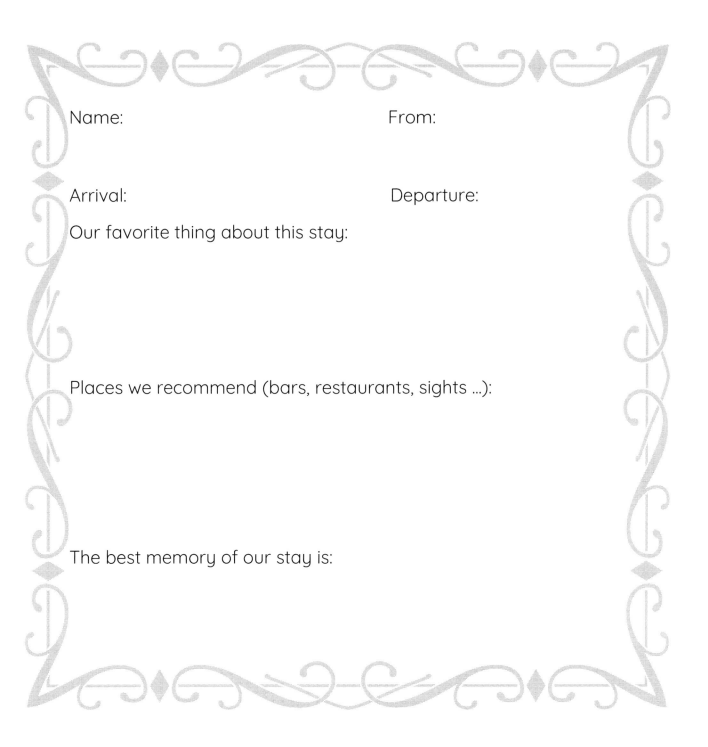

Name: From:

Arrival: Departure:

Our favorite thing about this stay:

Places we recommend (bars, restaurants, sights ...):

The best memory of our stay is:

Name: From:

Arrival: Departure:

Our favorite thing about this stay:

Places we recommend (bars, restaurants, sights ...):

The best memory of our stay is:

Name: From:

Arrival: Departure:

Our favorite thing about this stay:

Places we recommend (bars, restaurants, sights ...):

The best memory of our stay is:

Name: From:

Arrival: Departure:

Our favorite thing about this stay:

Places we recommend (bars, restaurants, sights ...):

The best memory of our stay is:

Name: From:

Arrival: Departure:

Our favorite thing about this stay:

Places we recommend (bars, restaurants, sights ...):

The best memory of our stay is:

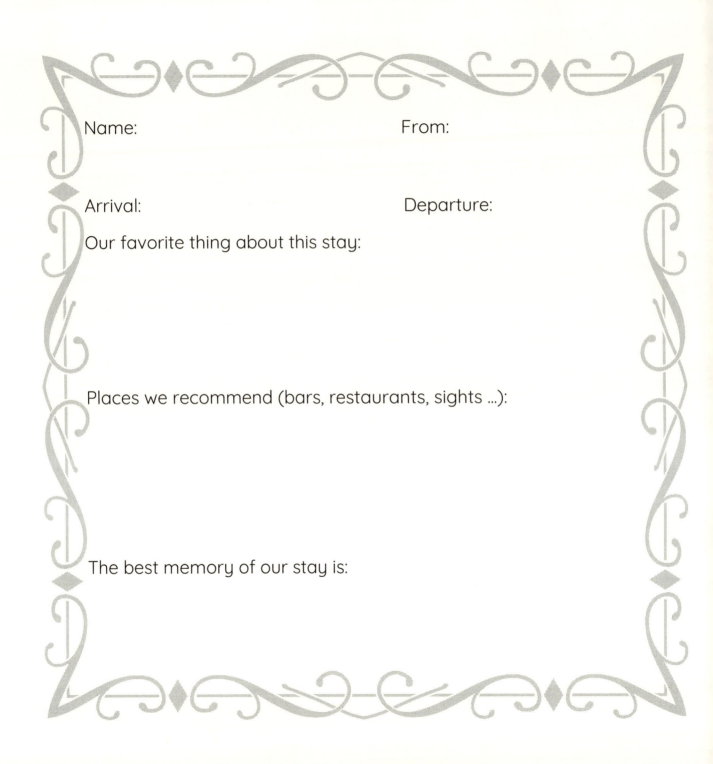

Name: From:

Arrival: Departure:

Our favorite thing about this stay:

Places we recommend (bars, restaurants, sights ...):

The best memory of our stay is:

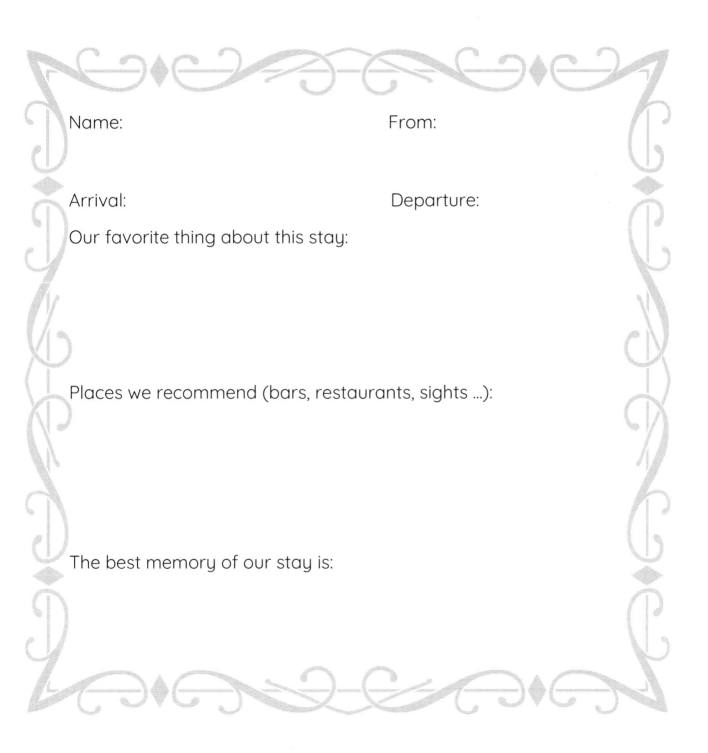

Name: From:

Arrival: Departure:

Our favorite thing about this stay:

Places we recommend (bars, restaurants, sights ...):

The best memory of our stay is:

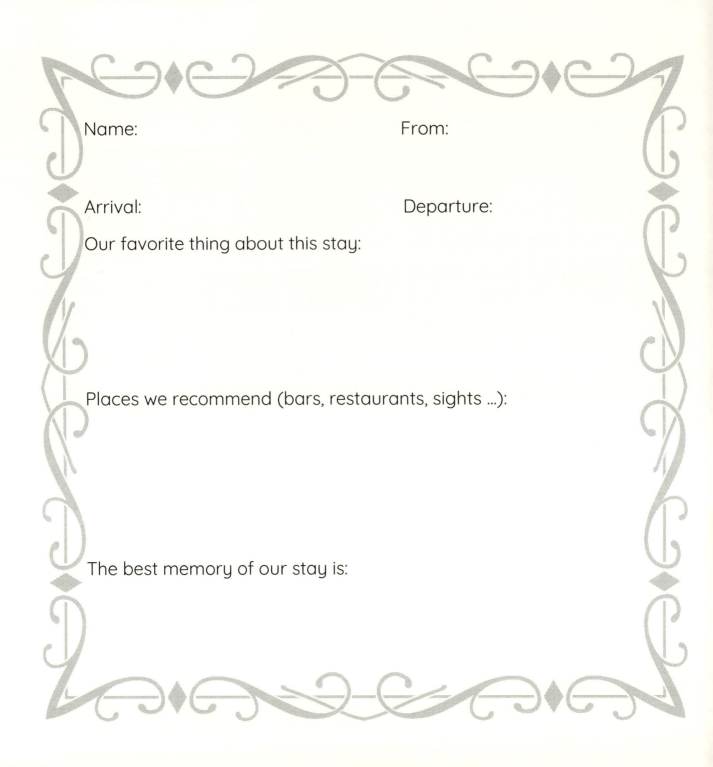

Name: From:

Arrival: Departure:

Our favorite thing about this stay:

Places we recommend (bars, restaurants, sights ...):

The best memory of our stay is:

Name: From:

Arrival: Departure:

Our favorite thing about this stay:

Places we recommend (bars, restaurants, sights ...):

The best memory of our stay is:

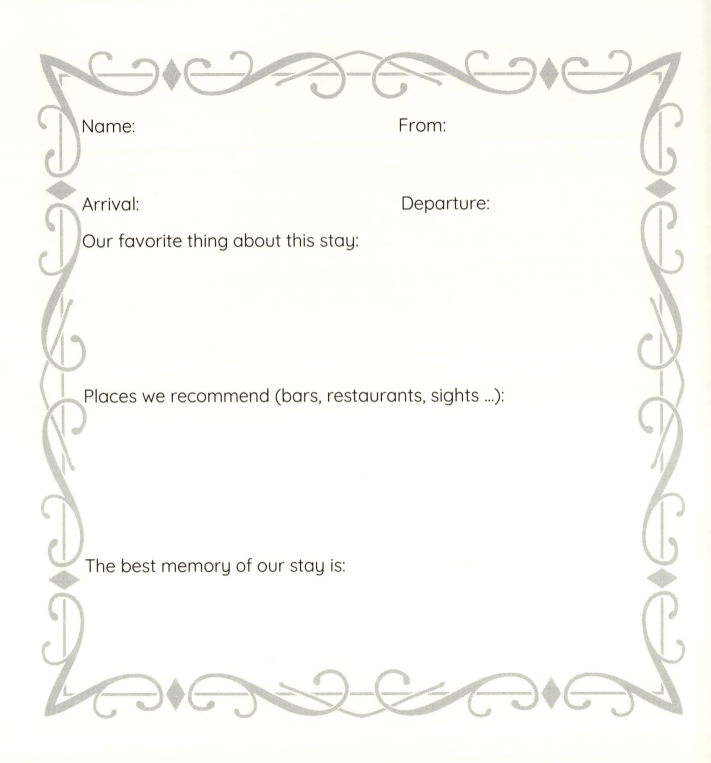

Name: From:

Arrival: Departure:

Our favorite thing about this stay:

Places we recommend (bars, restaurants, sights ...):

The best memory of our stay is:

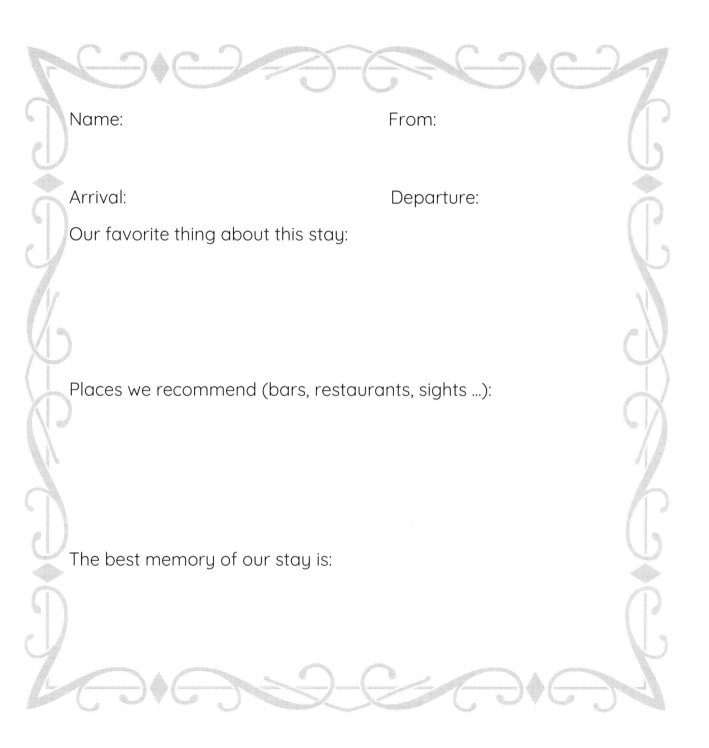

Name: From:

Arrival: Departure:

Our favorite thing about this stay:

Places we recommend (bars, restaurants, sights ...):

The best memory of our stay is:

Name: From:

Arrival: Departure:

Our favorite thing about this stay:

Places we recommend (bars, restaurants, sights ...):

The best memory of our stay is:

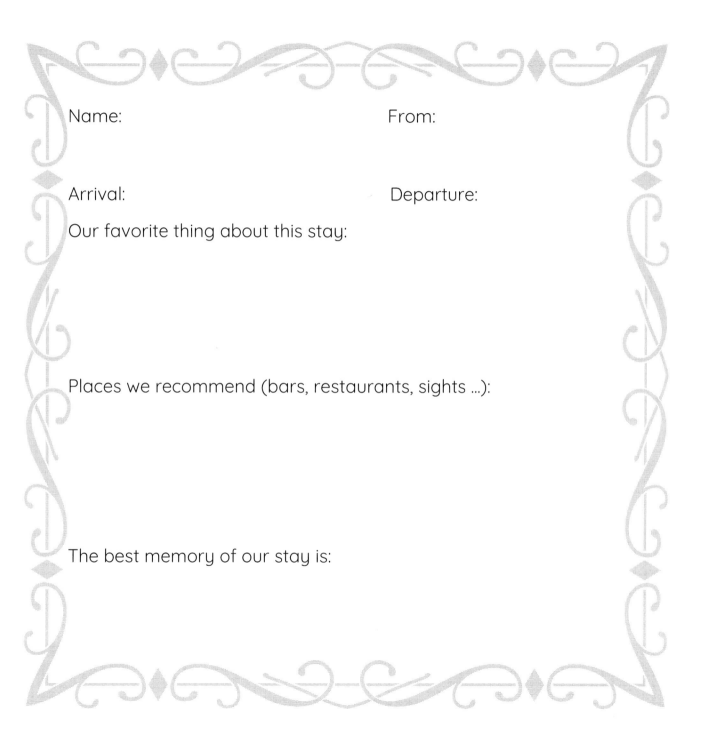

Name: From:

Arrival: Departure:

Our favorite thing about this stay:

Places we recommend (bars, restaurants, sights ...):

The best memory of our stay is:

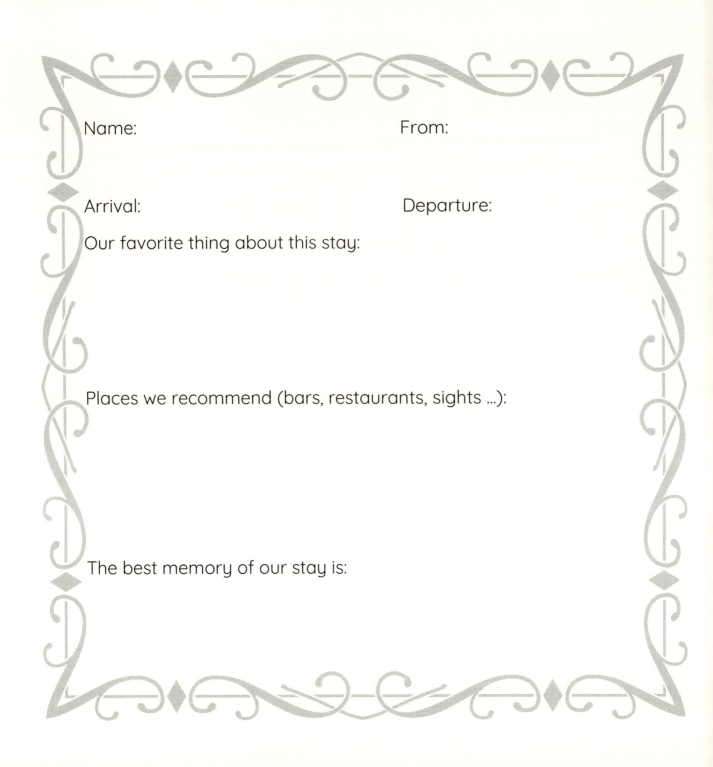

Name: From:

Arrival: Departure:

Our favorite thing about this stay:

Places we recommend (bars, restaurants, sights ...):

The best memory of our stay is:

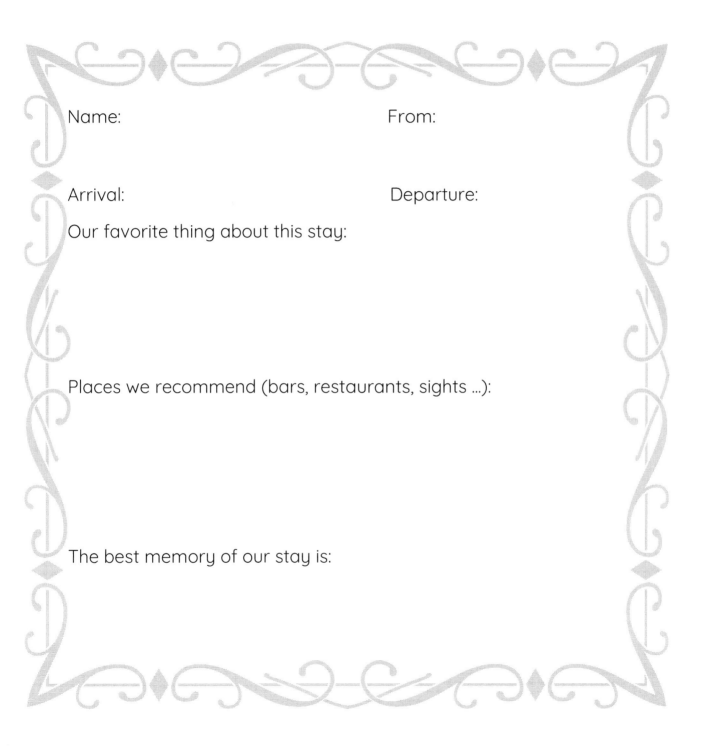

Name: From:

Arrival: Departure:

Our favorite thing about this stay:

Places we recommend (bars, restaurants, sights ...):

The best memory of our stay is:

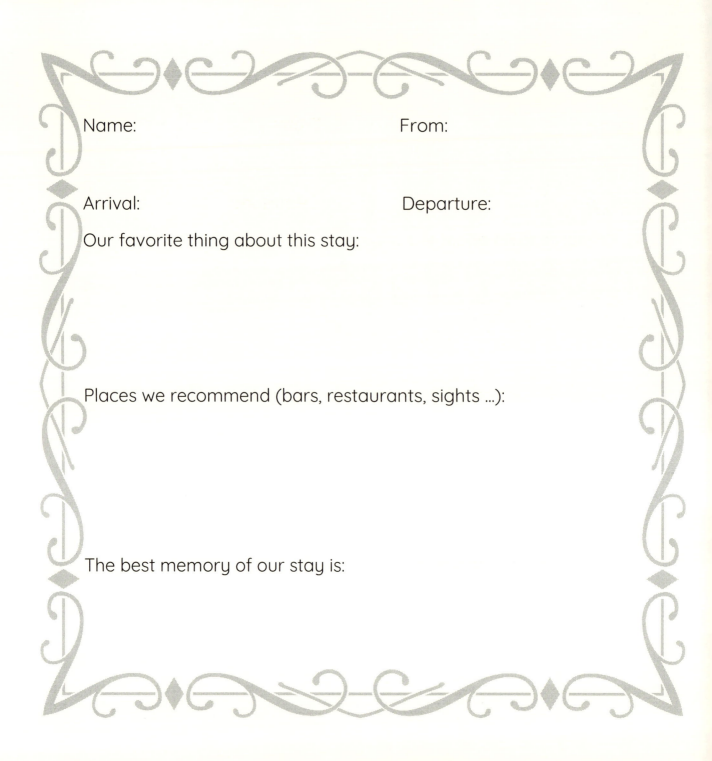

Name: From:

Arrival: Departure:

Our favorite thing about this stay:

Places we recommend (bars, restaurants, sights ...):

The best memory of our stay is:

Name: From:

Arrival: Departure:

Our favorite thing about this stay:

Places we recommend (bars, restaurants, sights ...):

The best memory of our stay is:

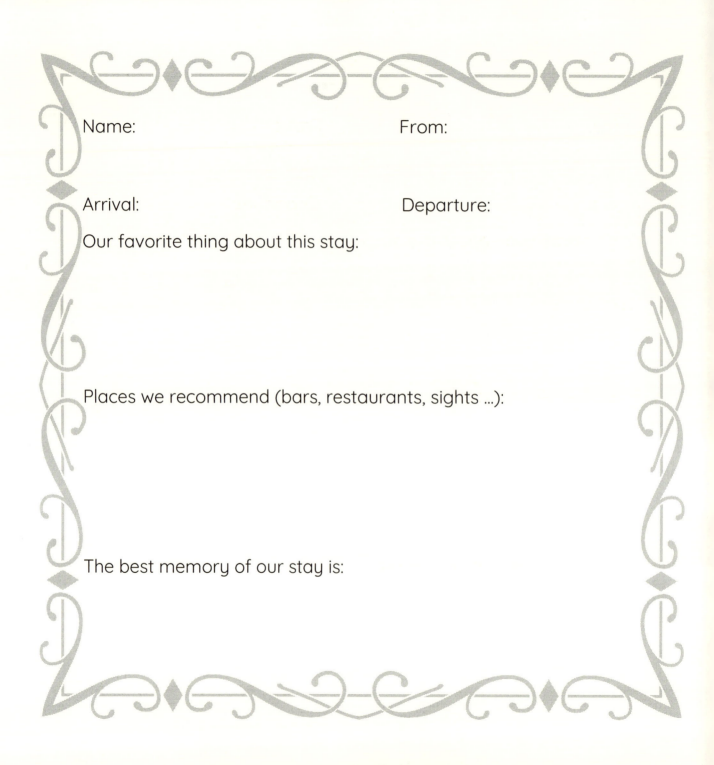

Name: From:

Arrival: Departure:

Our favorite thing about this stay:

Places we recommend (bars, restaurants, sights ...):

The best memory of our stay is:

Name: From:

Arrival: Departure:

Our favorite thing about this stay:

Places we recommend (bars, restaurants, sights ...):

The best memory of our stay is:

Name: From:

Arrival: Departure:

Our favorite thing about this stay:

Places we recommend (bars, restaurants, sights ...):

The best memory of our stay is:

Name: From:

Arrival: Departure:

Our favorite thing about this stay:

Places we recommend (bars, restaurants, sights ...):

The best memory of our stay is:

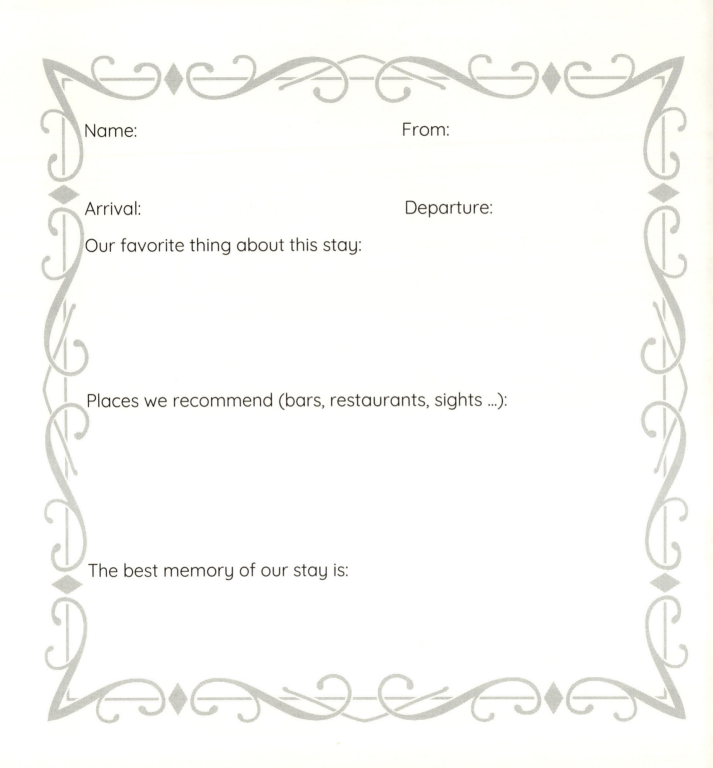

Name: From:

Arrival: Departure:

Our favorite thing about this stay:

Places we recommend (bars, restaurants, sights ...):

The best memory of our stay is:

Name: From:

Arrival: Departure:

Our favorite thing about this stay:

Places we recommend (bars, restaurants, sights ...):

The best memory of our stay is:

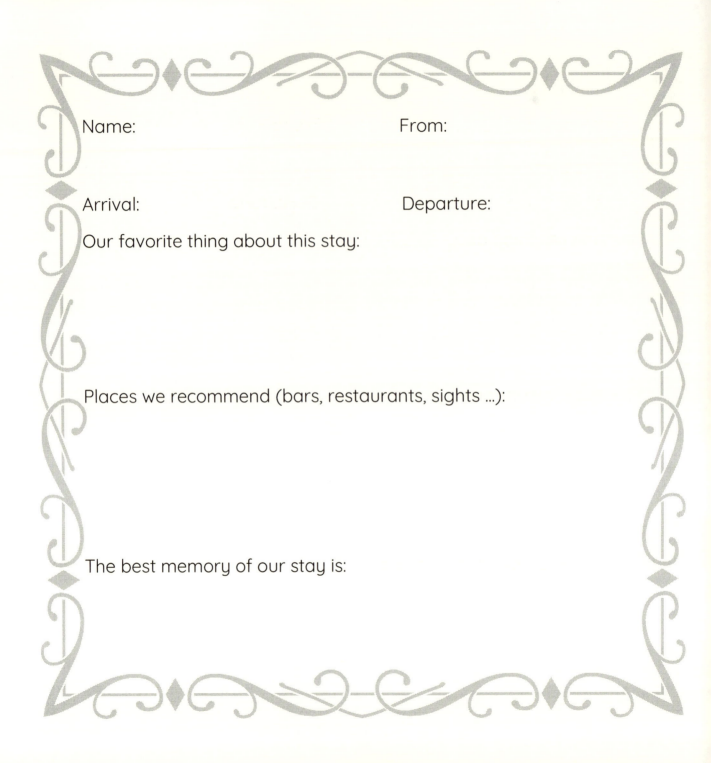

Name: From:

Arrival: Departure:

Our favorite thing about this stay:

Places we recommend (bars, restaurants, sights ...):

The best memory of our stay is:

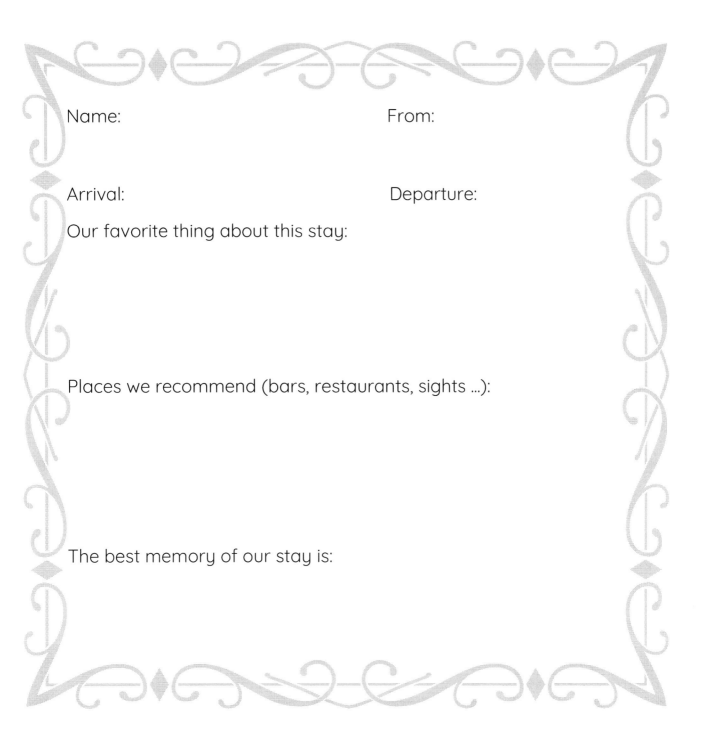

Name: From:

Arrival: Departure:

Our favorite thing about this stay:

Places we recommend (bars, restaurants, sights ...):

The best memory of our stay is:

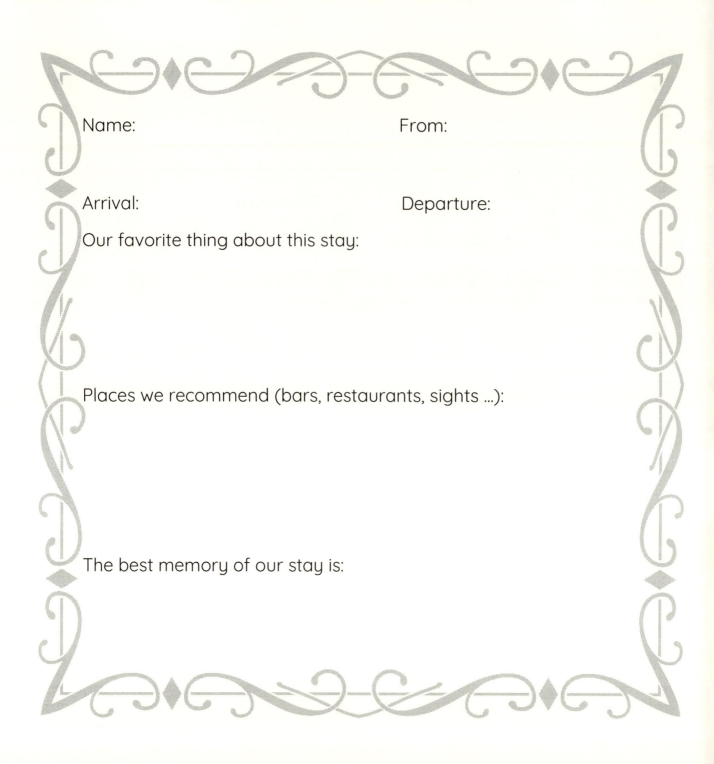

Name: From:

Arrival: Departure:

Our favorite thing about this stay:

Places we recommend (bars, restaurants, sights ...):

The best memory of our stay is:

Name: From:

Arrival: Departure:

Our favorite thing about this stay:

Places we recommend (bars, restaurants, sights ...):

The best memory of our stay is:

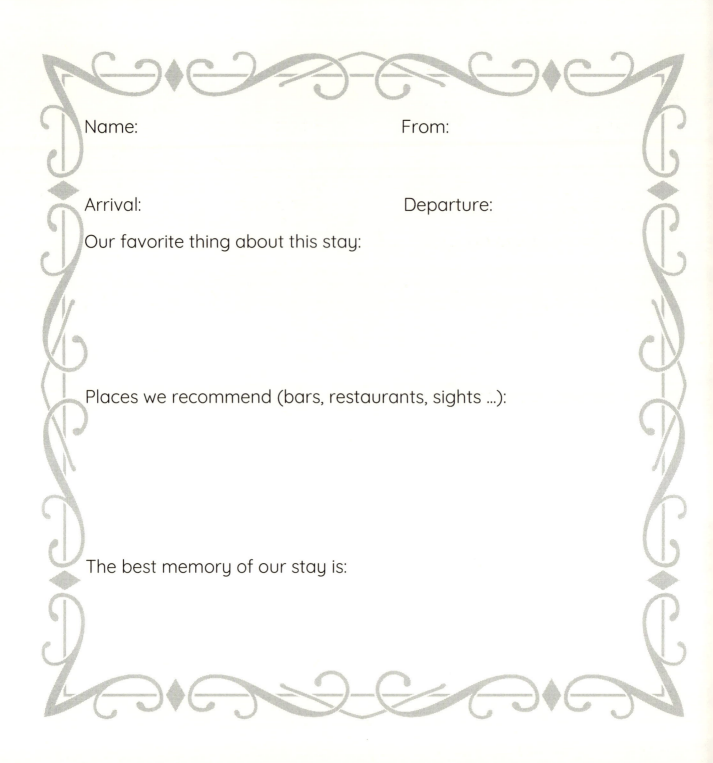

Name: From:

Arrival: Departure:

Our favorite thing about this stay:

Places we recommend (bars, restaurants, sights ...):

The best memory of our stay is:

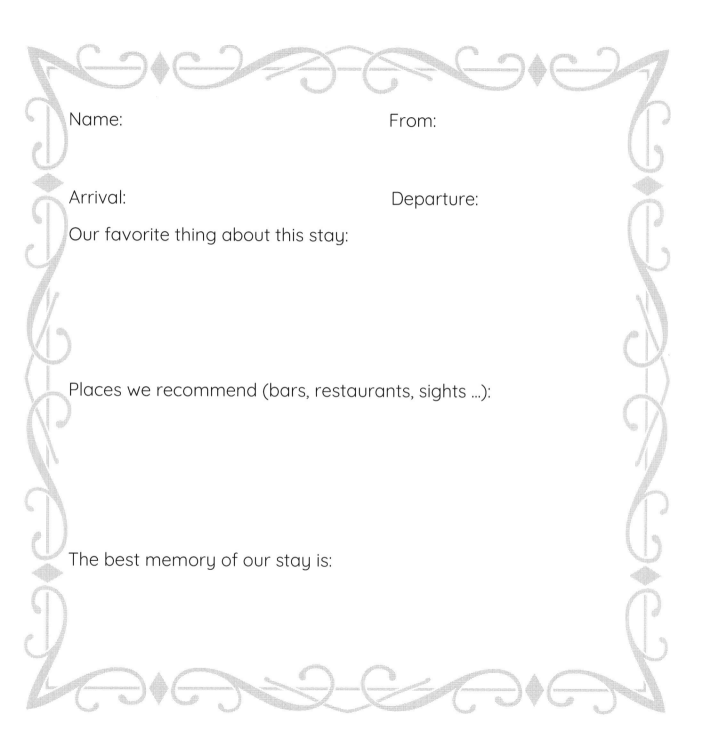

Name: From:

Arrival: Departure:

Our favorite thing about this stay:

Places we recommend (bars, restaurants, sights ...):

The best memory of our stay is:

Name: From:

Arrival: Departure:

Our favorite thing about this stay:

Places we recommend (bars, restaurants, sights ...):

The best memory of our stay is:

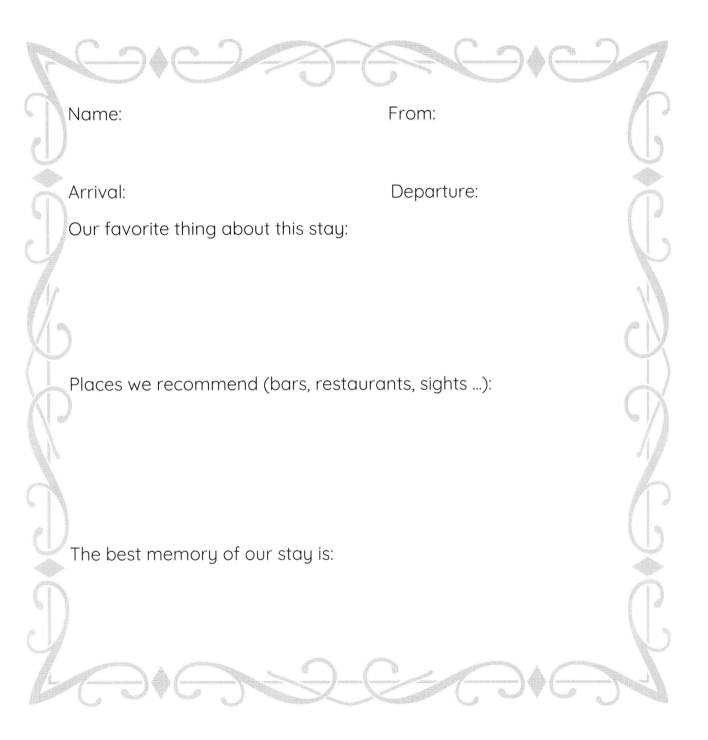

Name: From:

Arrival: Departure:

Our favorite thing about this stay:

Places we recommend (bars, restaurants, sights ...):

The best memory of our stay is:

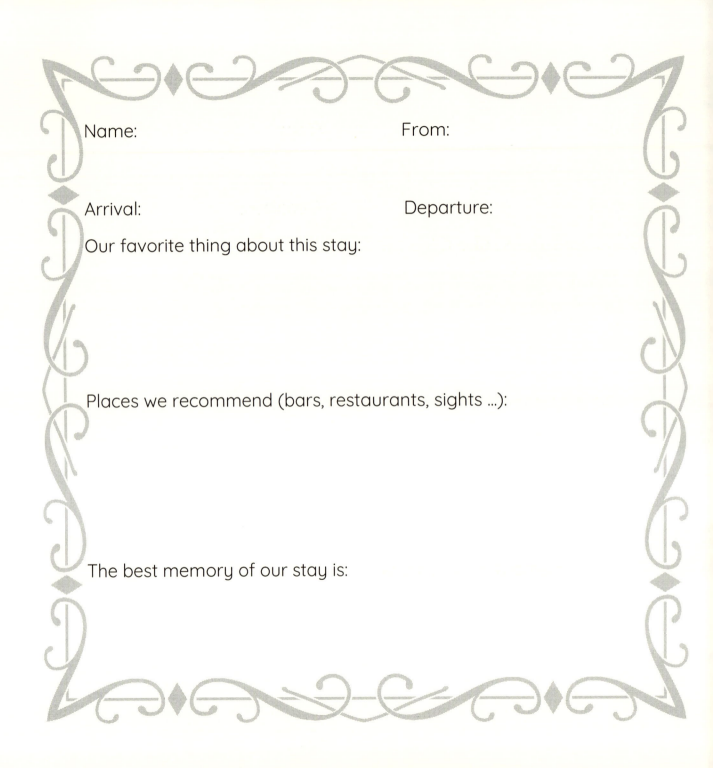

Name: From:

Arrival: Departure:

Our favorite thing about this stay:

Places we recommend (bars, restaurants, sights ...):

The best memory of our stay is:

Name: From:

Arrival: Departure:

Our favorite thing about this stay:

Places we recommend (bars, restaurants, sights ...):

The best memory of our stay is:

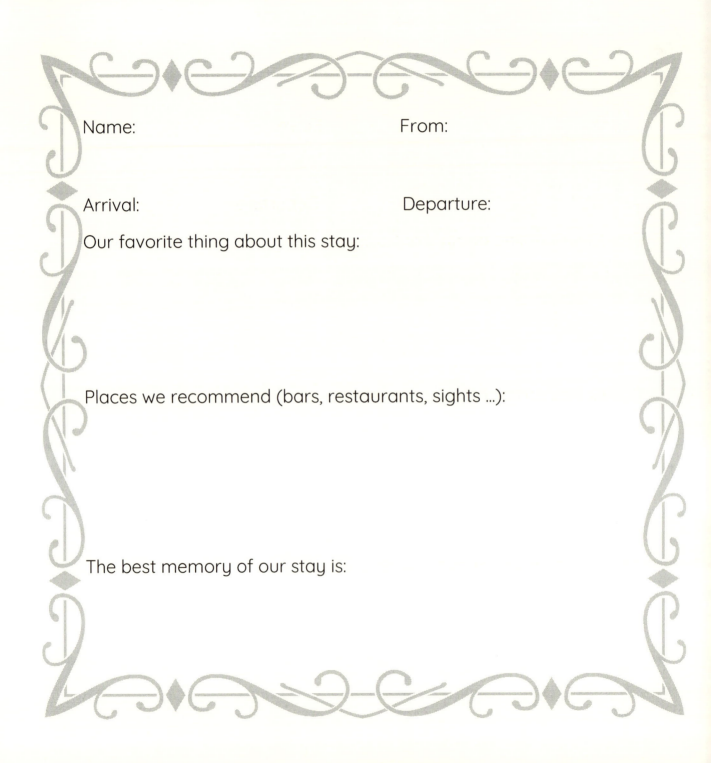

Name: From:

Arrival: Departure:

Our favorite thing about this stay:

Places we recommend (bars, restaurants, sights ...):

The best memory of our stay is:

Name: From:

Arrival: Departure:

Our favorite thing about this stay:

Places we recommend (bars, restaurants, sights ...):

The best memory of our stay is:

Name: From:

Arrival: Departure:

Our favorite thing about this stay:

Places we recommend (bars, restaurants, sights ...):

The best memory of our stay is:

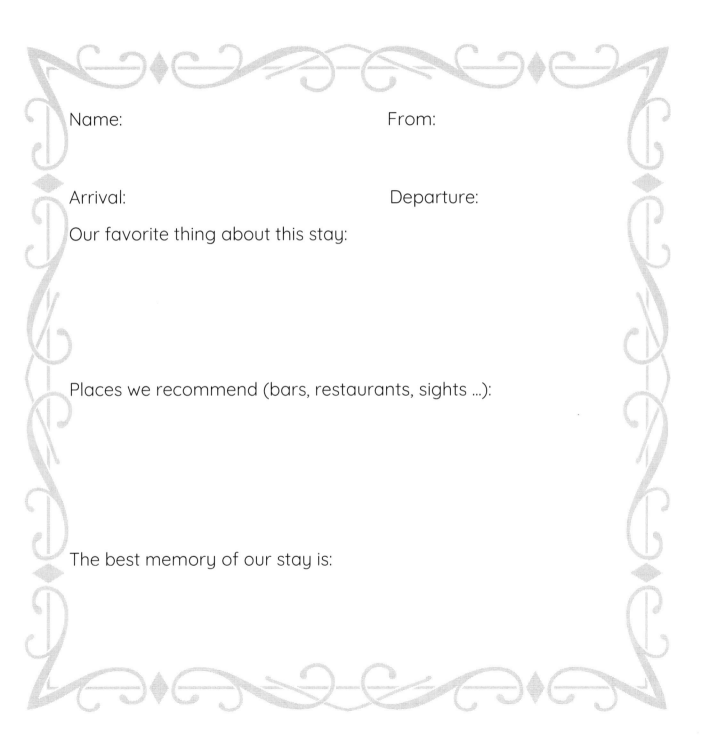

Name: From:

Arrival: Departure:

Our favorite thing about this stay:

Places we recommend (bars, restaurants, sights ...):

The best memory of our stay is:

Name: From:

Arrival: Departure:

Our favorite thing about this stay:

Places we recommend (bars, restaurants, sights ...):

The best memory of our stay is:

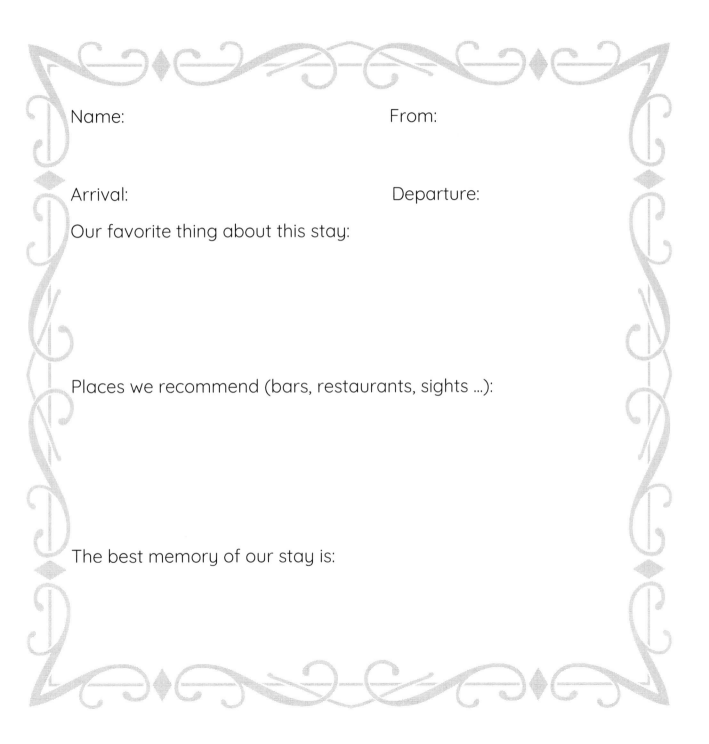

Name: From:

Arrival: Departure:

Our favorite thing about this stay:

Places we recommend (bars, restaurants, sights ...):

The best memory of our stay is:

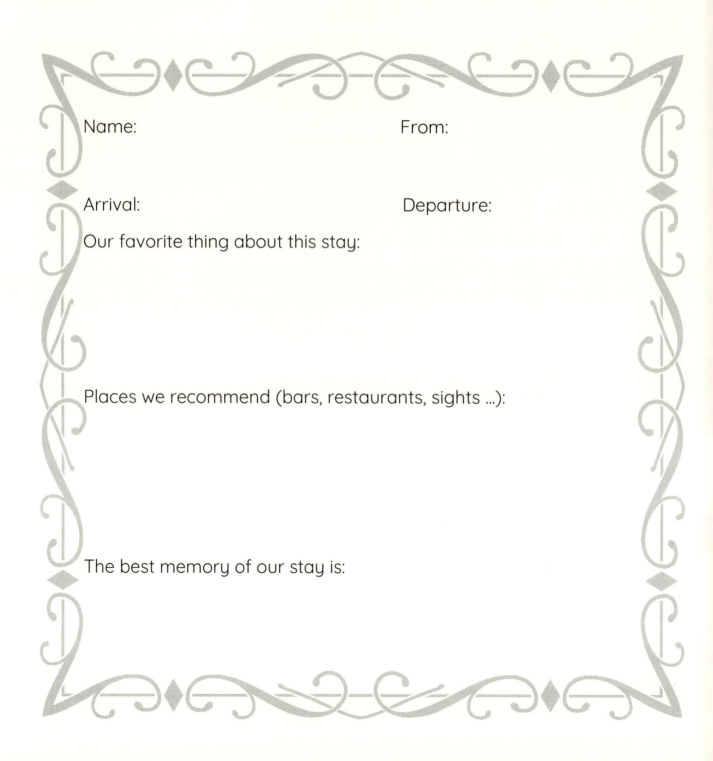

Name: From:

Arrival: Departure:

Our favorite thing about this stay:

Places we recommend (bars, restaurants, sights ...):

The best memory of our stay is:

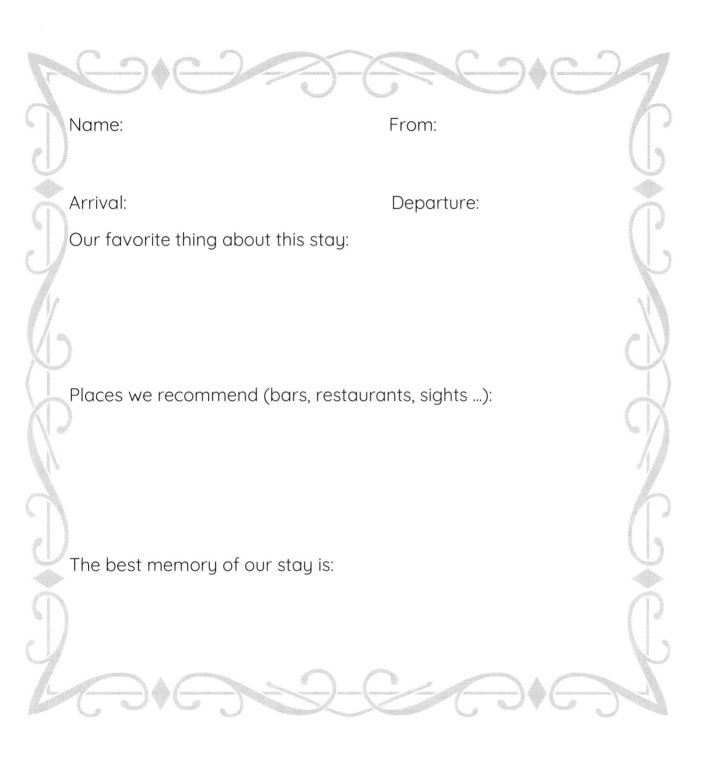

Name: From:

Arrival: Departure:

Our favorite thing about this stay:

Places we recommend (bars, restaurants, sights ...):

The best memory of our stay is:

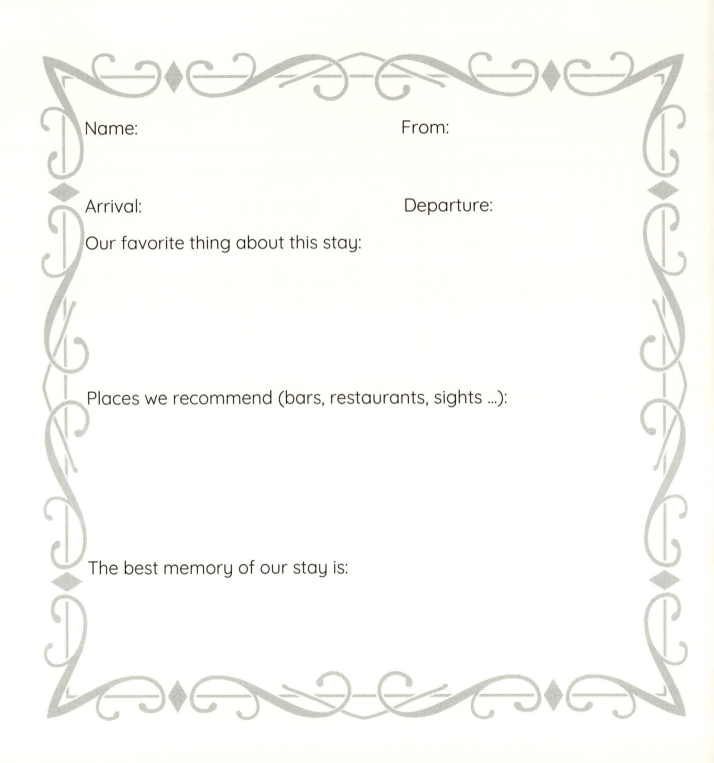

Name: From:

Arrival: Departure:

Our favorite thing about this stay:

Places we recommend (bars, restaurants, sights ...):

The best memory of our stay is:

Name: From:

Arrival: Departure:

Our favorite thing about this stay:

Places we recommend (bars, restaurants, sights ...):

The best memory of our stay is:

Name: From:

Arrival: Departure:

Our favorite thing about this stay:

Places we recommend (bars, restaurants, sights ...):

The best memory of our stay is:

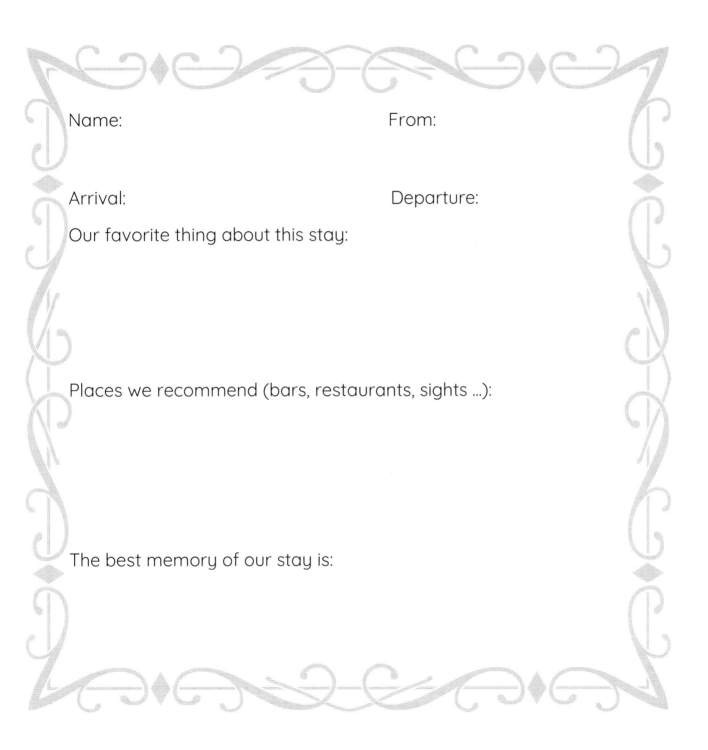

Name: From:

Arrival: Departure:

Our favorite thing about this stay:

Places we recommend (bars, restaurants, sights ...):

The best memory of our stay is:

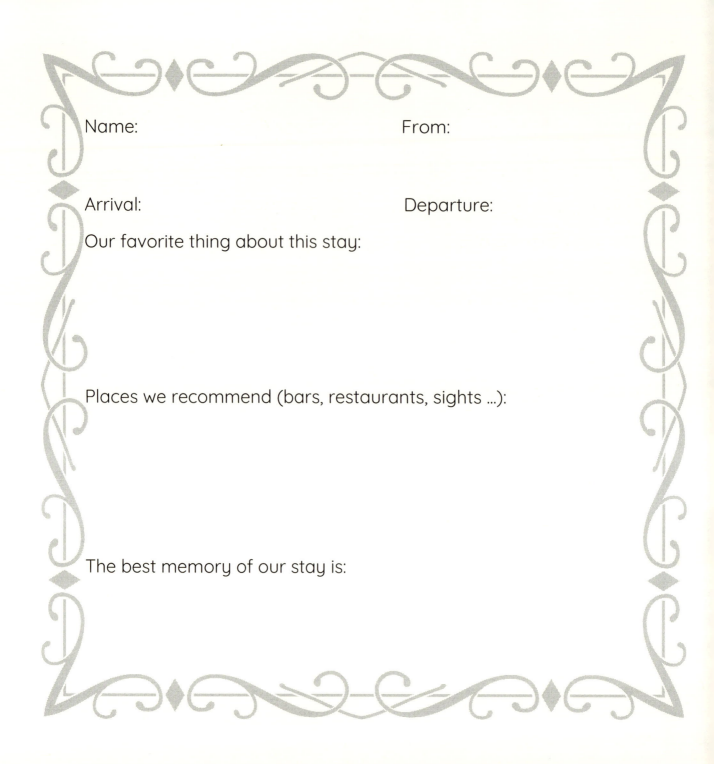

Name: From:

Arrival: Departure:

Our favorite thing about this stay:

Places we recommend (bars, restaurants, sights ...):

The best memory of our stay is:

Name: From:

Arrival: Departure:

Our favorite thing about this stay:

Places we recommend (bars, restaurants, sights ...):

The best memory of our stay is:

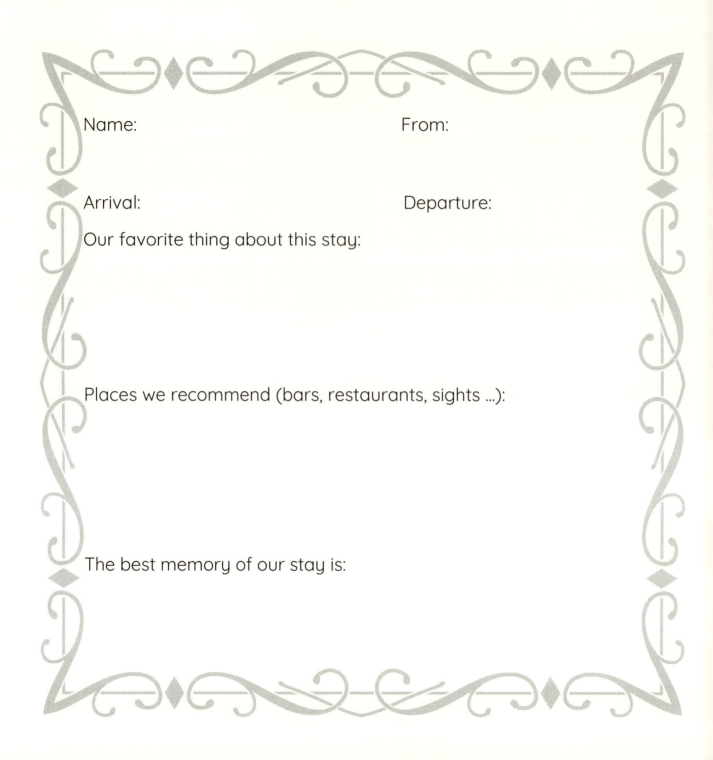

Name: From:

Arrival: Departure:

Our favorite thing about this stay:

Places we recommend (bars, restaurants, sights ...):

The best memory of our stay is:

Name: From:

Arrival: Departure:

Our favorite thing about this stay:

Places we recommend (bars, restaurants, sights ...):

The best memory of our stay is:

Name: From:

Arrival: Departure:

Our favorite thing about this stay:

Places we recommend (bars, restaurants, sights ...):

The best memory of our stay is:

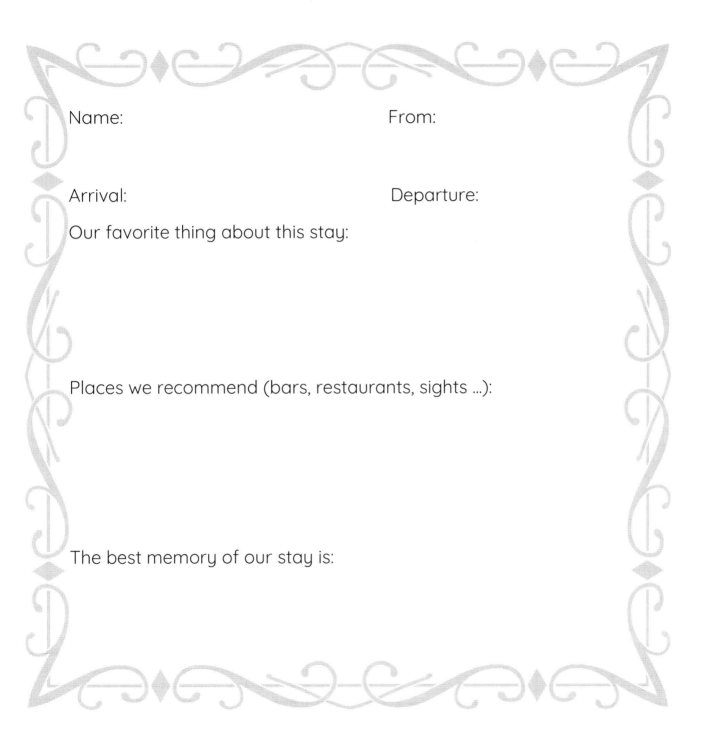

Name: From:

Arrival: Departure:

Our favorite thing about this stay:

Places we recommend (bars, restaurants, sights ...):

The best memory of our stay is:

Name: From:

Arrival: Departure:

Our favorite thing about this stay:

Places we recommend (bars, restaurants, sights ...):

The best memory of our stay is:

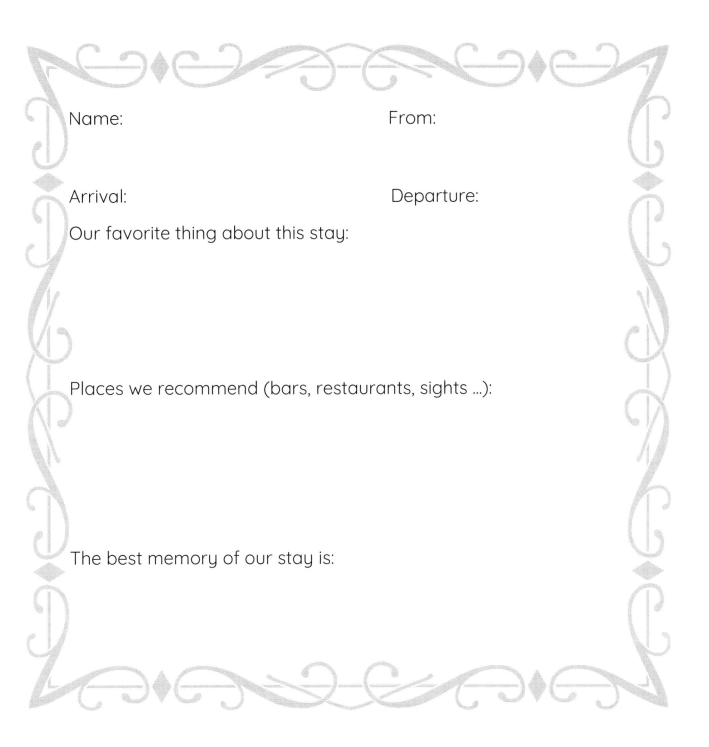

Name: From:

Arrival: Departure:

Our favorite thing about this stay:

Places we recommend (bars, restaurants, sights ...):

The best memory of our stay is:

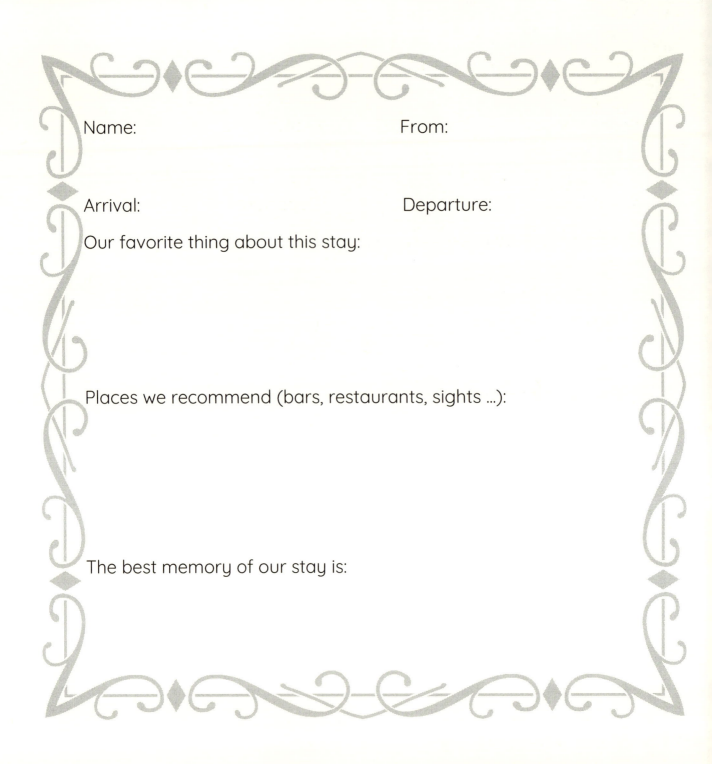

Name: From:

Arrival: Departure:

Our favorite thing about this stay:

Places we recommend (bars, restaurants, sights ...):

The best memory of our stay is:

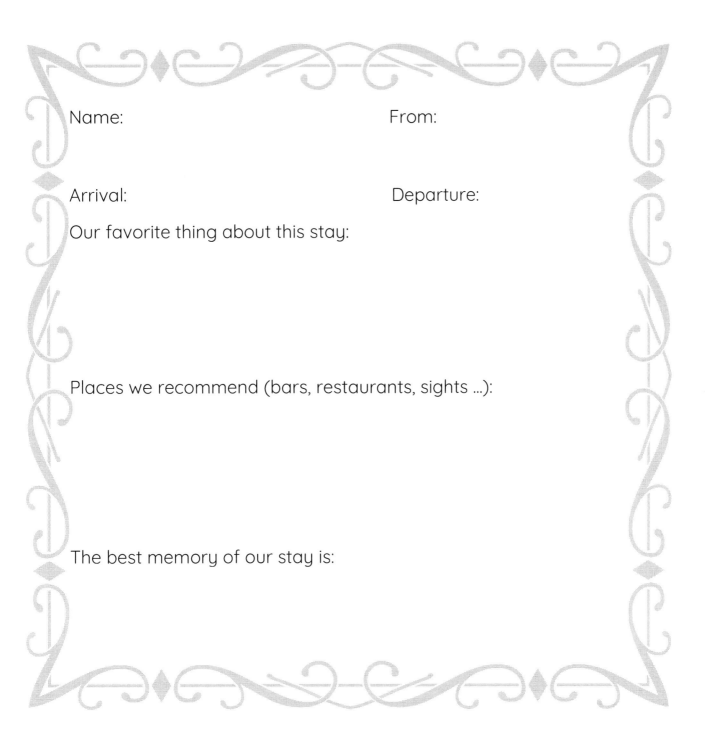

Name: From:

Arrival: Departure:

Our favorite thing about this stay:

Places we recommend (bars, restaurants, sights ...):

The best memory of our stay is:

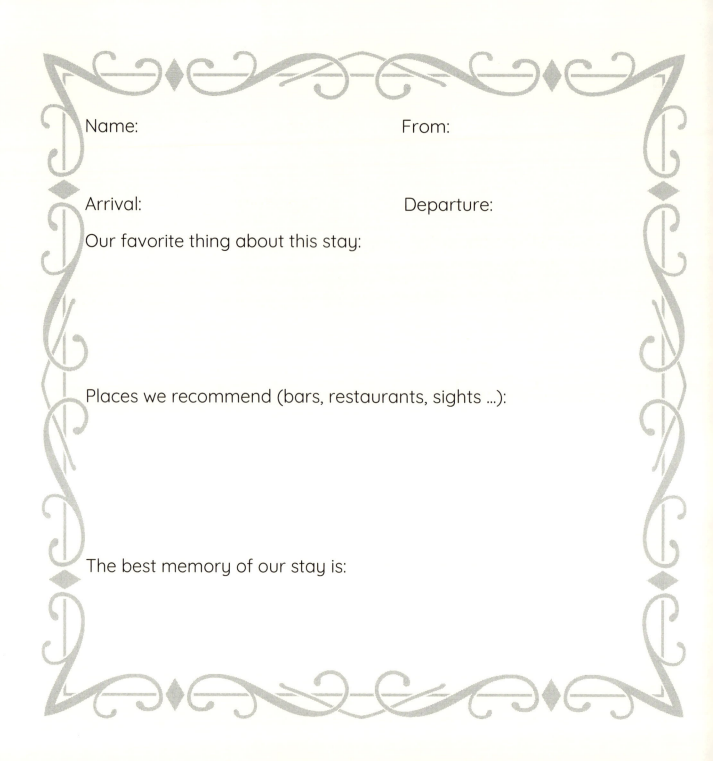

Name: From:

Arrival: Departure:

Our favorite thing about this stay:

Places we recommend (bars, restaurants, sights ...):

The best memory of our stay is:

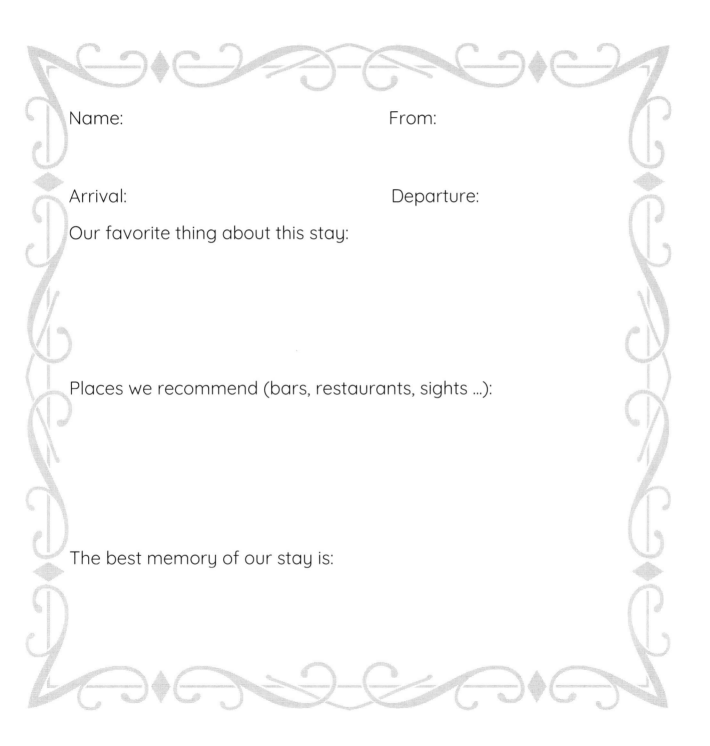

Name: From:

Arrival: Departure:

Our favorite thing about this stay:

Places we recommend (bars, restaurants, sights ...):

The best memory of our stay is:

Name: From:

Arrival: Departure:

Our favorite thing about this stay:

Places we recommend (bars, restaurants, sights ...):

The best memory of our stay is:

Name: From:

Arrival: Departure:

Our favorite thing about this stay:

Places we recommend (bars, restaurants, sights ...):

The best memory of our stay is:

Name: From:

Arrival: Departure:

Our favorite thing about this stay:

Places we recommend (bars, restaurants, sights ...):

The best memory of our stay is:

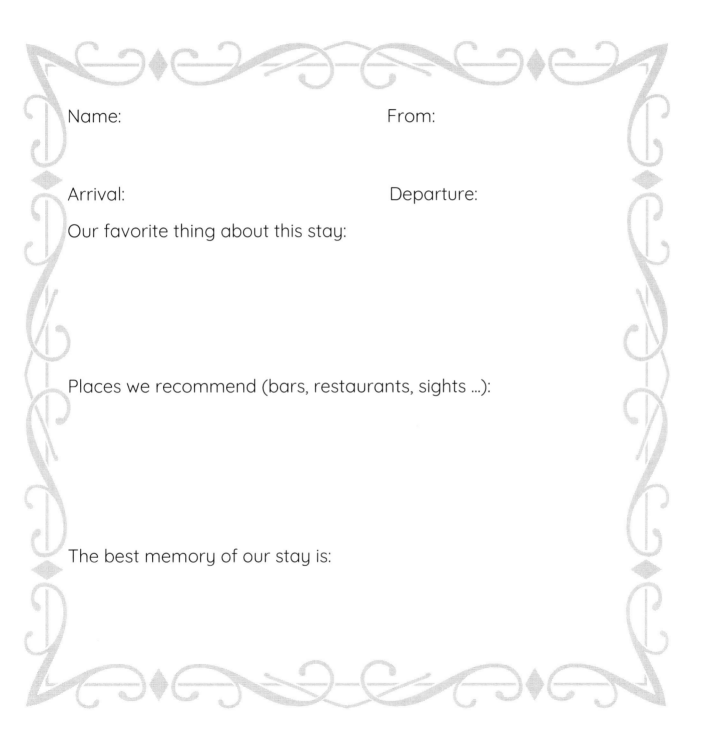

Name: From:

Arrival: Departure:

Our favorite thing about this stay:

Places we recommend (bars, restaurants, sights …):

The best memory of our stay is:

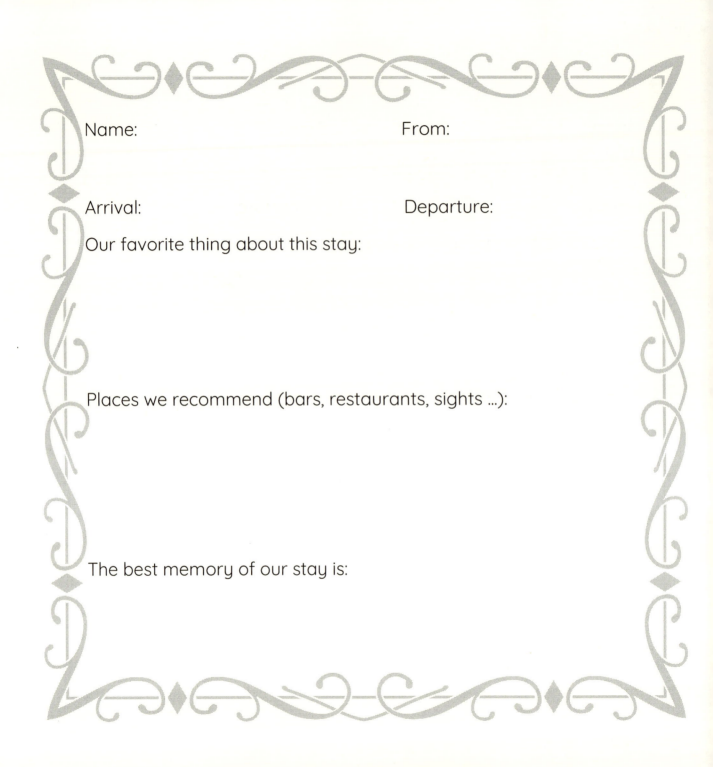

Name: From:

Arrival: Departure:

Our favorite thing about this stay:

Places we recommend (bars, restaurants, sights ...):

The best memory of our stay is:

Name: From:

Arrival: Departure:

Our favorite thing about this stay:

Places we recommend (bars, restaurants, sights ...):

The best memory of our stay is:

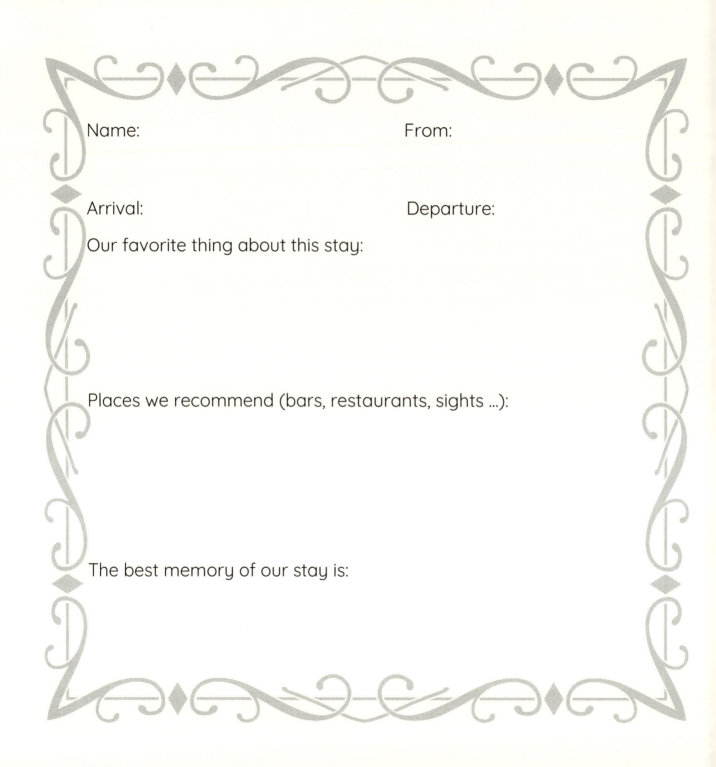

Name: From:

Arrival: Departure:

Our favorite thing about this stay:

Places we recommend (bars, restaurants, sights ...):

The best memory of our stay is:

Name: From:

Arrival: Departure:

Our favorite thing about this stay:

Places we recommend (bars, restaurants, sights ...):

The best memory of our stay is:

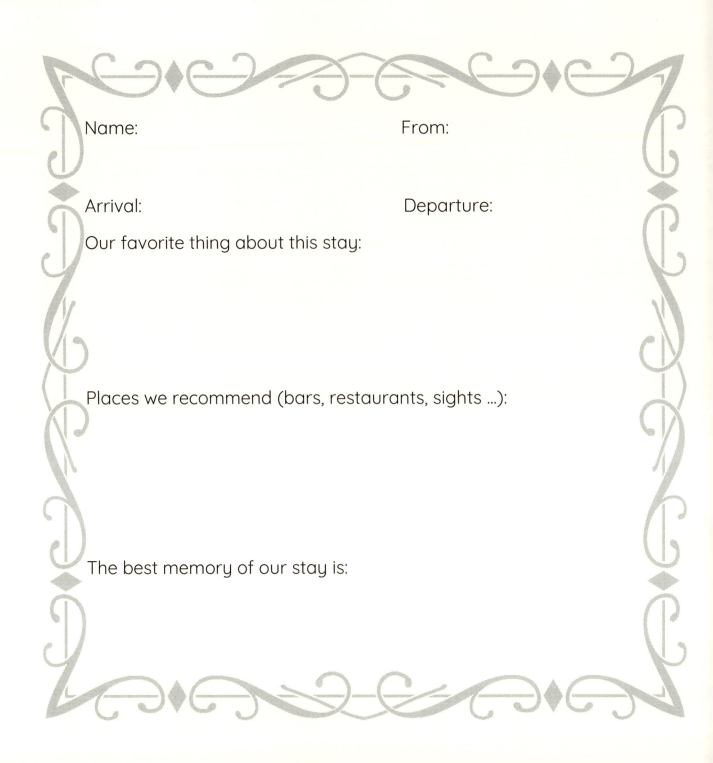

Name: From:

Arrival: Departure:

Our favorite thing about this stay:

Places we recommend (bars, restaurants, sights ...):

The best memory of our stay is:

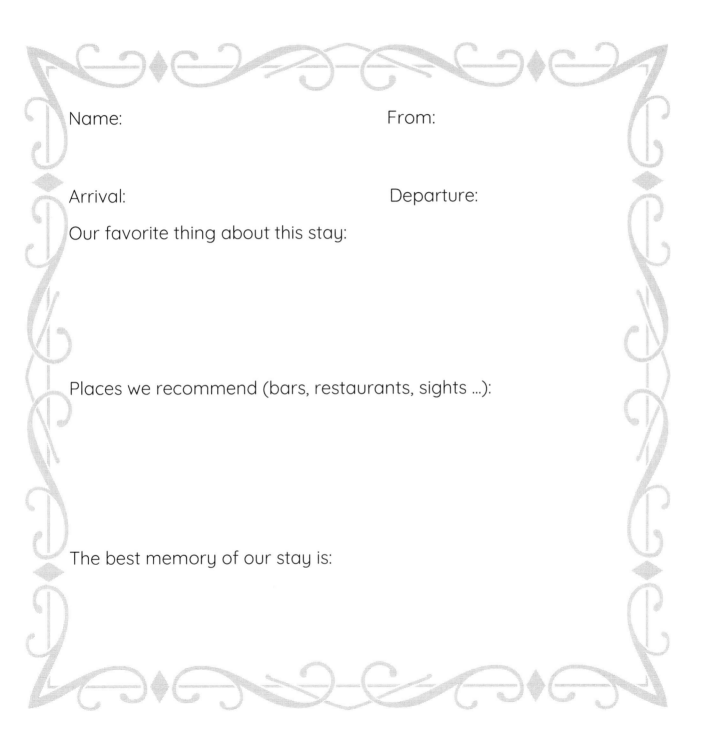

Name: From:

Arrival: Departure:

Our favorite thing about this stay:

Places we recommend (bars, restaurants, sights ...):

The best memory of our stay is:

Name: From:

Arrival: Departure:

Our favorite thing about this stay:

Places we recommend (bars, restaurants, sights ...):

The best memory of our stay is:

Name: From:

Arrival: Departure:

Our favorite thing about this stay:

Places we recommend (bars, restaurants, sights ...):

The best memory of our stay is:

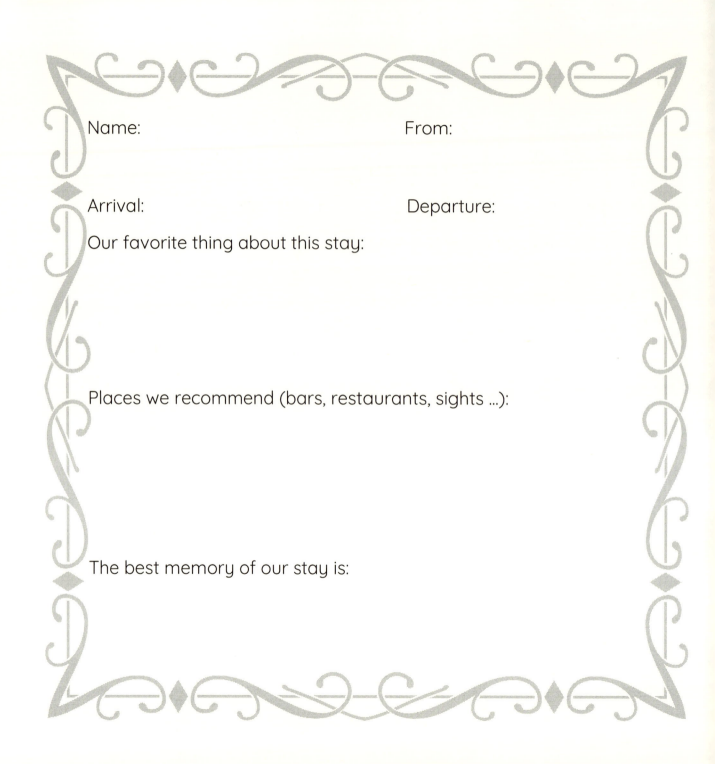

Name: From:

Arrival: Departure:

Our favorite thing about this stay:

Places we recommend (bars, restaurants, sights ...):

The best memory of our stay is:

Name: From:

Arrival: Departure:

Our favorite thing about this stay:

Places we recommend (bars, restaurants, sights ...):

The best memory of our stay is:

Name: From:

Arrival: Departure:

Our favorite thing about this stay:

Places we recommend (bars, restaurants, sights ...):

The best memory of our stay is:

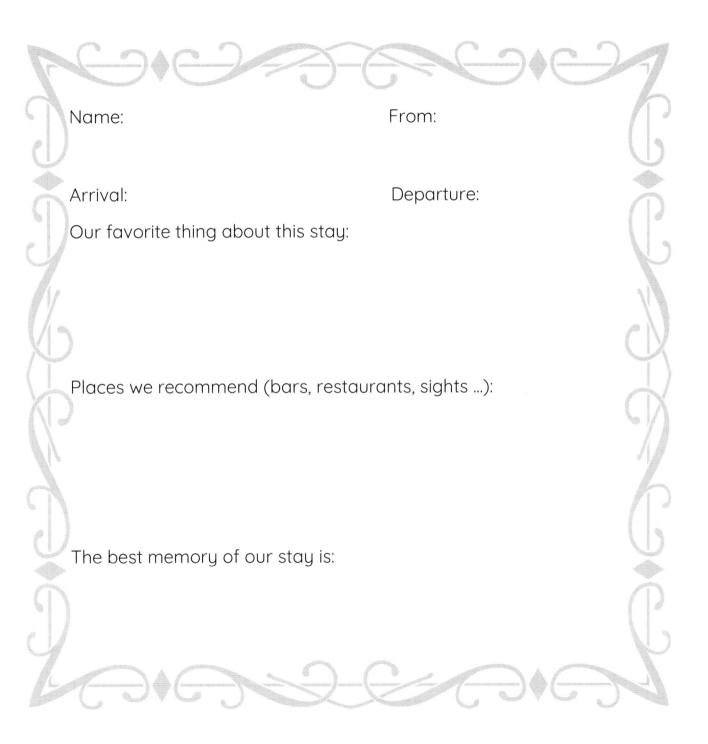

Name: From:

Arrival: Departure:

Our favorite thing about this stay:

Places we recommend (bars, restaurants, sights ...):

The best memory of our stay is:

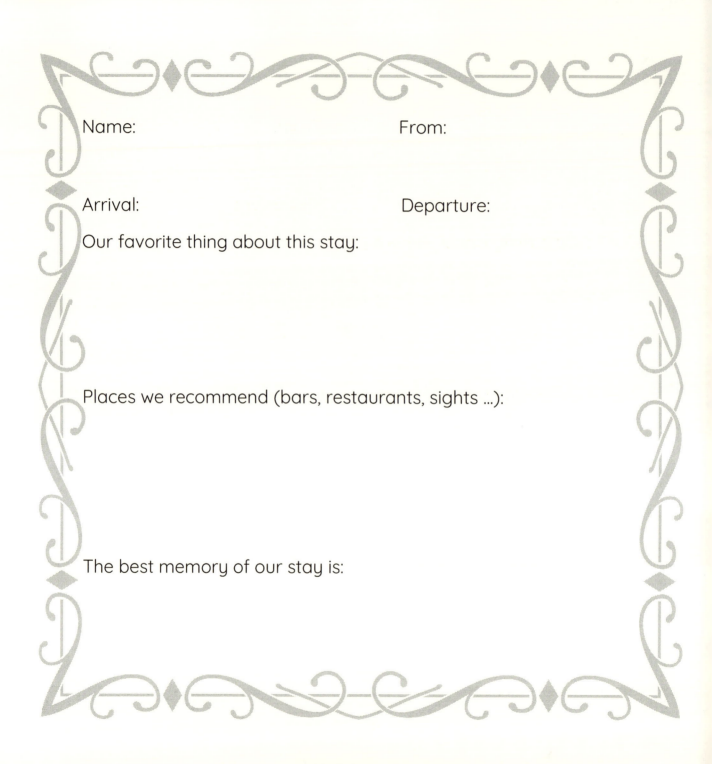

Name: From:

Arrival: Departure:

Our favorite thing about this stay:

Places we recommend (bars, restaurants, sights ...):

The best memory of our stay is:

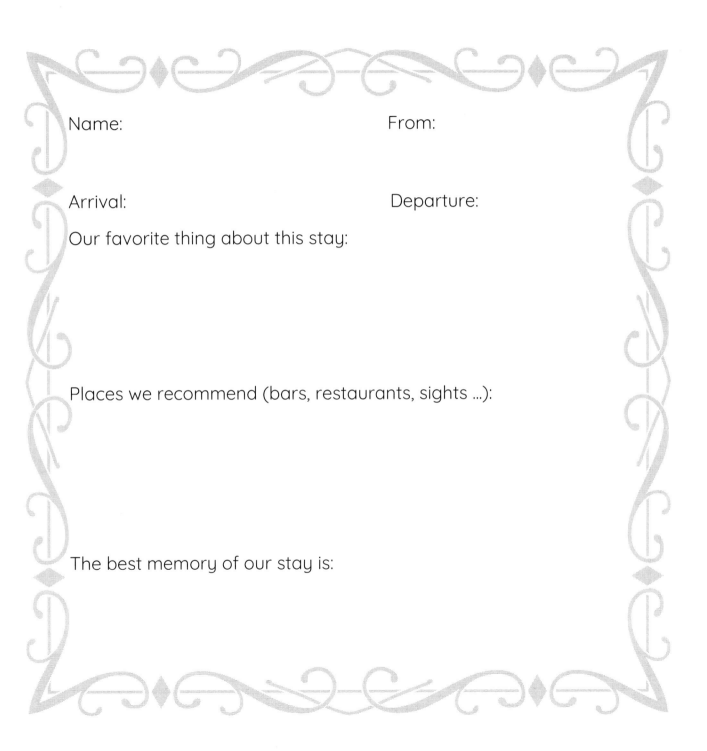

Name: From:

Arrival: Departure:

Our favorite thing about this stay:

Places we recommend (bars, restaurants, sights ...):

The best memory of our stay is:

Name: From:

Arrival: Departure:

Our favorite thing about this stay:

Places we recommend (bars, restaurants, sights ...):

The best memory of our stay is:

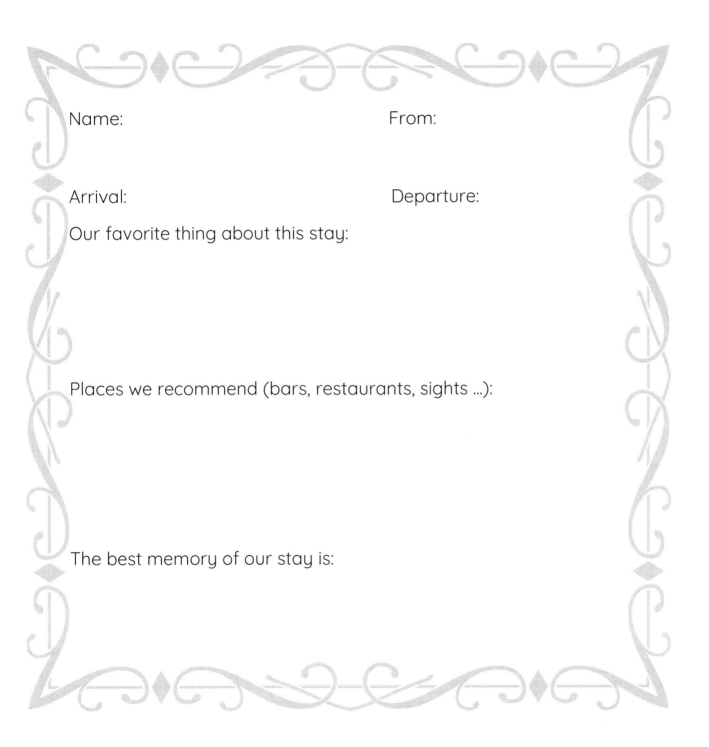

Name: From:

Arrival: Departure:

Our favorite thing about this stay:

Places we recommend (bars, restaurants, sights ...):

The best memory of our stay is:

Name: From:

Arrival: Departure:

Our favorite thing about this stay:

Places we recommend (bars, restaurants, sights ...):

The best memory of our stay is:

Name: From:

Arrival: Departure:

Our favorite thing about this stay:

Places we recommend (bars, restaurants, sights ...):

The best memory of our stay is:

Name: From:

Arrival: Departure:

Our favorite thing about this stay:

Places we recommend (bars, restaurants, sights ...):

The best memory of our stay is:

Name: From:

Arrival: Departure:

Our favorite thing about this stay:

Places we recommend (bars, restaurants, sights ...):

The best memory of our stay is:

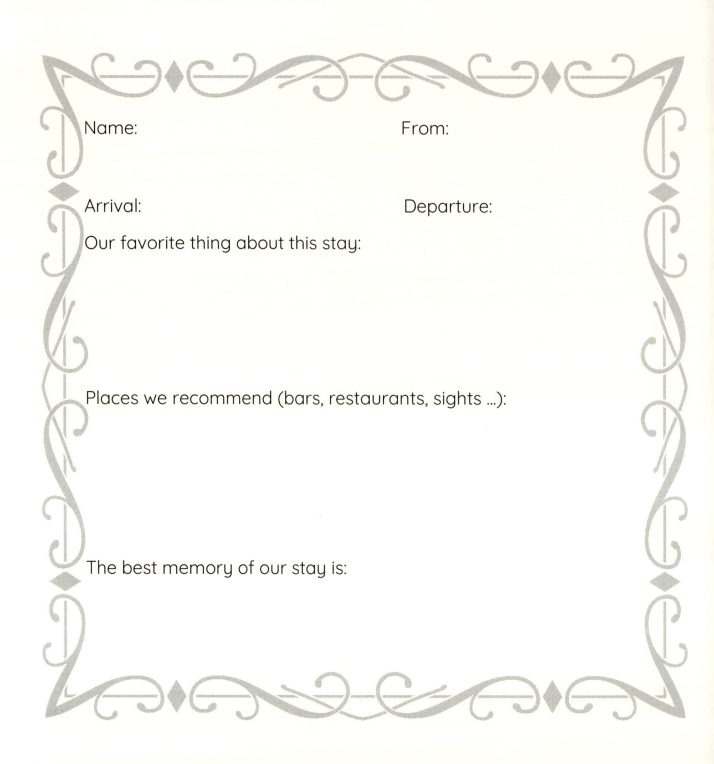

Name: From:

Arrival: Departure:

Our favorite thing about this stay:

Places we recommend (bars, restaurants, sights ...):

The best memory of our stay is:

Name: From:

Arrival: Departure:

Our favorite thing about this stay:

Places we recommend (bars, restaurants, sights ...):

The best memory of our stay is:

Name: From:

Arrival: Departure:

Our favorite thing about this stay:

Places we recommend (bars, restaurants, sights ...):

The best memory of our stay is:

Name: From:

Arrival: Departure:

Our favorite thing about this stay:

Places we recommend (bars, restaurants, sights ...):

The best memory of our stay is:

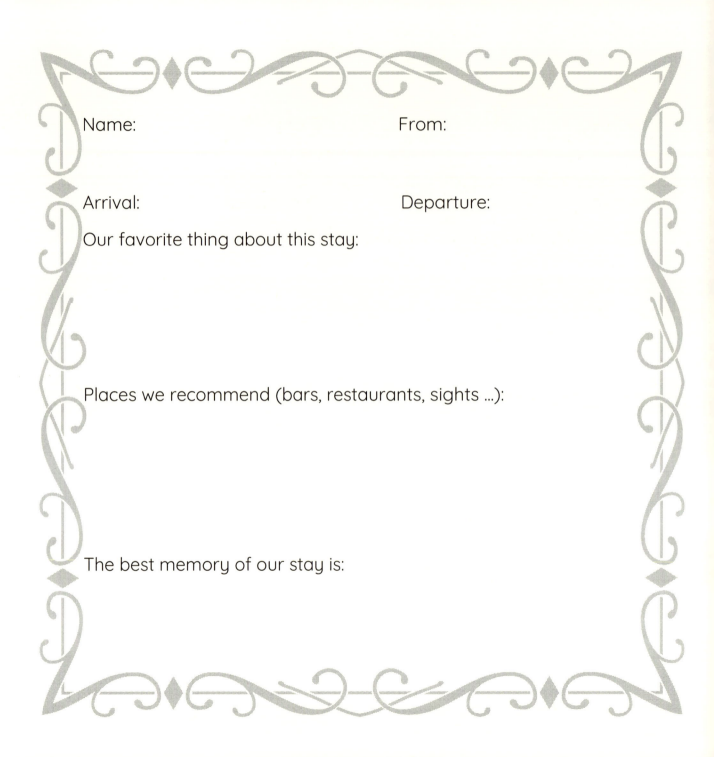

Name: From:

Arrival: Departure:

Our favorite thing about this stay:

Places we recommend (bars, restaurants, sights ...):

The best memory of our stay is:

Name: From:

Arrival: Departure:

Our favorite thing about this stay:

Places we recommend (bars, restaurants, sights ...):

The best memory of our stay is:

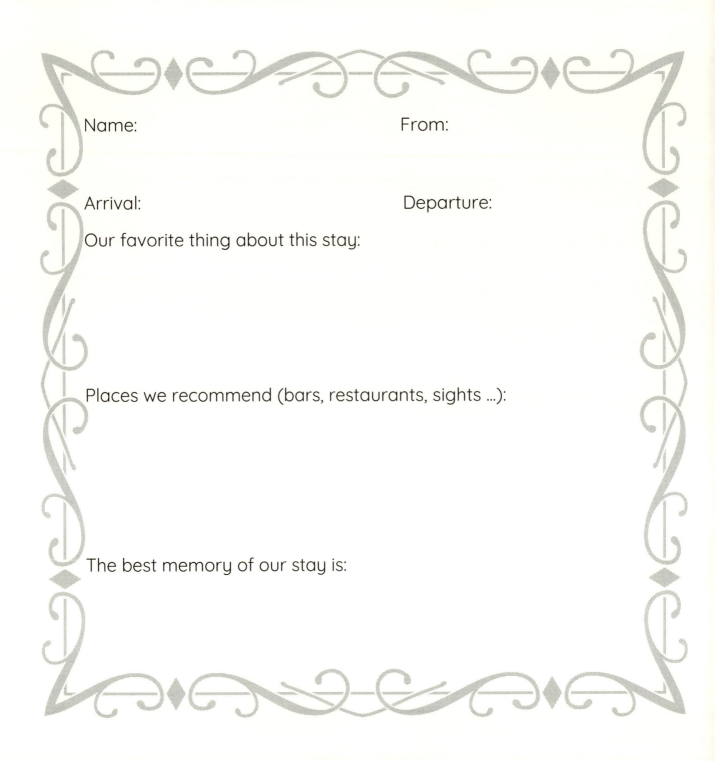

Name: From:

Arrival: Departure:

Our favorite thing about this stay:

Places we recommend (bars, restaurants, sights ...):

The best memory of our stay is:

Name: From:

Arrival: Departure:

Our favorite thing about this stay:

Places we recommend (bars, restaurants, sights ...):

The best memory of our stay is:

Name: From:

Arrival: Departure:

Our favorite thing about this stay:

Places we recommend (bars, restaurants, sights ...):

The best memory of our stay is:

Name: From:

Arrival: Departure:

Our favorite thing about this stay:

Places we recommend (bars, restaurants, sights ...):

The best memory of our stay is:

Name: From:

Arrival: Departure:

Our favorite thing about this stay:

Places we recommend (bars, restaurants, sights ...):

The best memory of our stay is:

Name: From:

Arrival: Departure:

Our favorite thing about this stay:

Places we recommend (bars, restaurants, sights ...):

The best memory of our stay is:

Name: From:

Arrival: Departure:

Our favorite thing about this stay:

Places we recommend (bars, restaurants, sights ...):

The best memory of our stay is:

Name: From:

Arrival: Departure:

Our favorite thing about this stay:

Places we recommend (bars, restaurants, sights ...):

The best memory of our stay is:

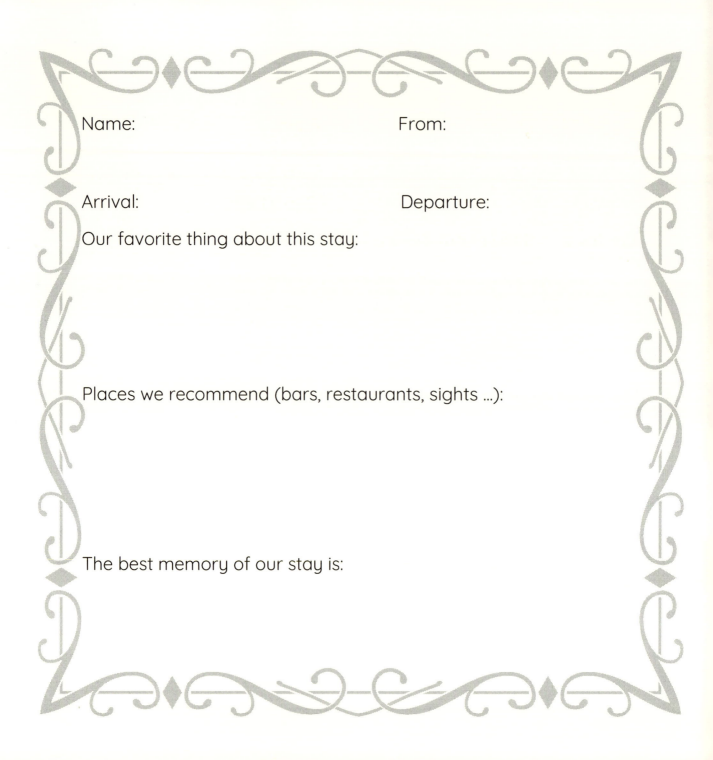

Name: From:

Arrival: Departure:

Our favorite thing about this stay:

Places we recommend (bars, restaurants, sights ...):

The best memory of our stay is:

Name: From:

Arrival: Departure:

Our favorite thing about this stay:

Places we recommend (bars, restaurants, sights ...):

The best memory of our stay is:

Name: From:

Arrival: Departure:

Our favorite thing about this stay:

Places we recommend (bars, restaurants, sights ...):

The best memory of our stay is:

Name: From:

Arrival: Departure:

Our favorite thing about this stay:

Places we recommend (bars, restaurants, sights ...):

The best memory of our stay is:

Name: From:

Arrival: Departure:

Our favorite thing about this stay:

Places we recommend (bars, restaurants, sights ...):

The best memory of our stay is:

Name: From:

Arrival: Departure:

Our favorite thing about this stay:

Places we recommend (bars, restaurants, sights ...):

The best memory of our stay is:

Name: From:

Arrival: Departure:

Our favorite thing about this stay:

Places we recommend (bars, restaurants, sights ...):

The best memory of our stay is:

Name: From:

Arrival: Departure:

Our favorite thing about this stay:

Places we recommend (bars, restaurants, sights ...):

The best memory of our stay is:

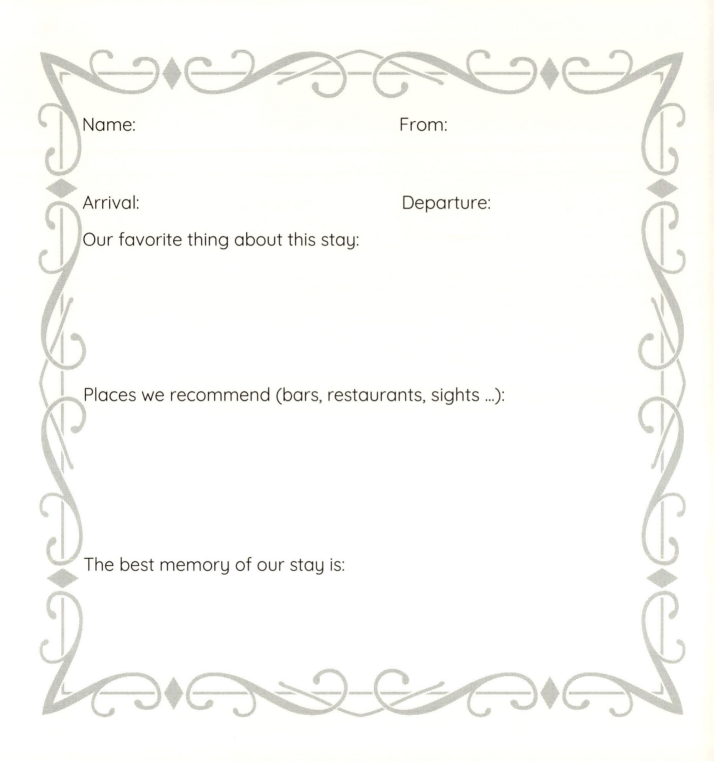

Name: From:

Arrival: Departure:

Our favorite thing about this stay:

Places we recommend (bars, restaurants, sights ...):

The best memory of our stay is:

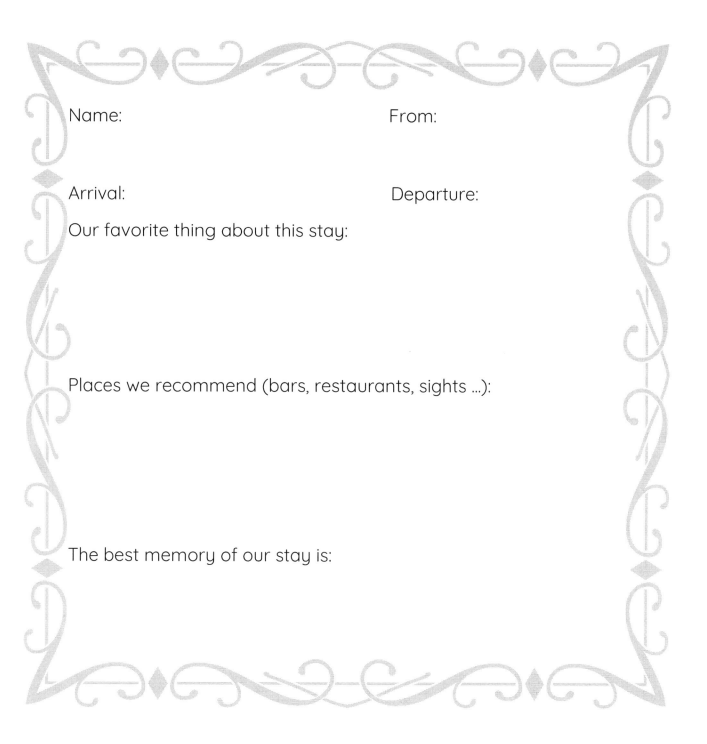

Name: From:

Arrival: Departure:

Our favorite thing about this stay:

Places we recommend (bars, restaurants, sights ...):

The best memory of our stay is:

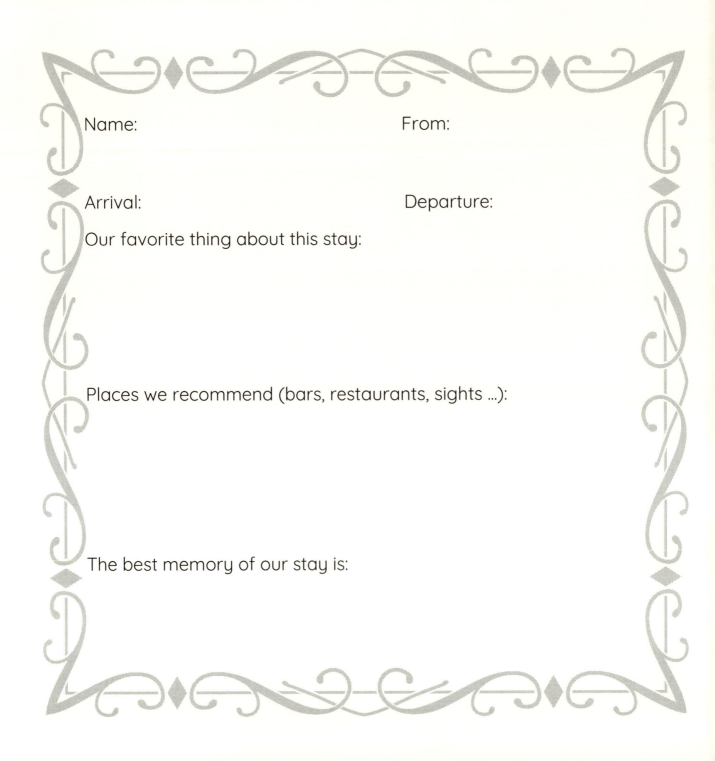

Name: From:

Arrival: Departure:

Our favorite thing about this stay:

Places we recommend (bars, restaurants, sights ...):

The best memory of our stay is:

Name: From:

Arrival: Departure:

Our favorite thing about this stay:

Places we recommend (bars, restaurants, sights ...):

The best memory of our stay is:

Name: From:

Arrival: Departure:

Our favorite thing about this stay:

Places we recommend (bars, restaurants, sights ...):

The best memory of our stay is:

Name: From:

Arrival: Departure:

Our favorite thing about this stay:

Places we recommend (bars, restaurants, sights ...):

The best memory of our stay is:

Name: From:

Arrival: Departure:

Our favorite thing about this stay:

Places we recommend (bars, restaurants, sights ...):

The best memory of our stay is:

Name: From:

Arrival: Departure:

Our favorite thing about this stay:

Places we recommend (bars, restaurants, sights ...):

The best memory of our stay is:

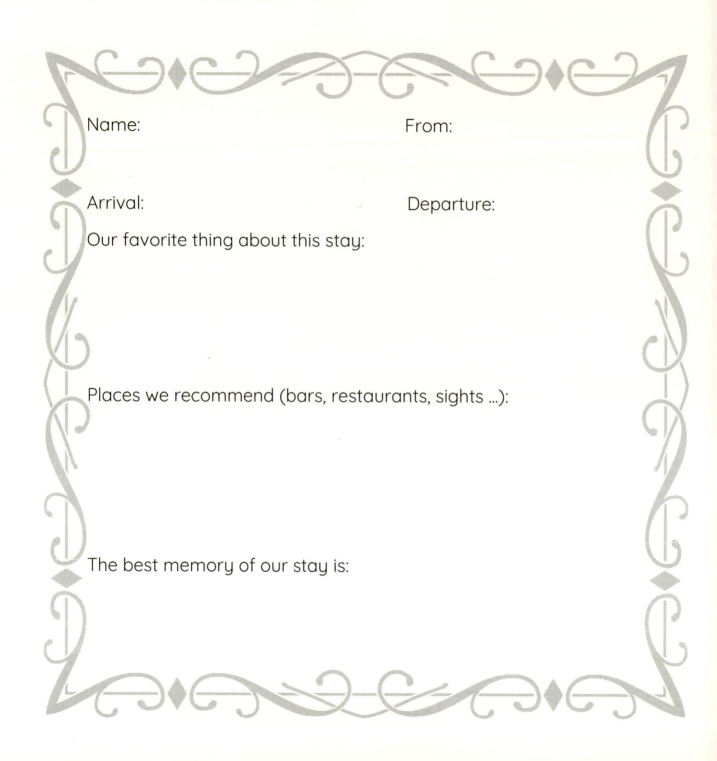

Name: From:

Arrival: Departure:

Our favorite thing about this stay:

Places we recommend (bars, restaurants, sights ...):

The best memory of our stay is:

Name: From:

Arrival: Departure:

Our favorite thing about this stay:

Places we recommend (bars, restaurants, sights ...):

The best memory of our stay is:

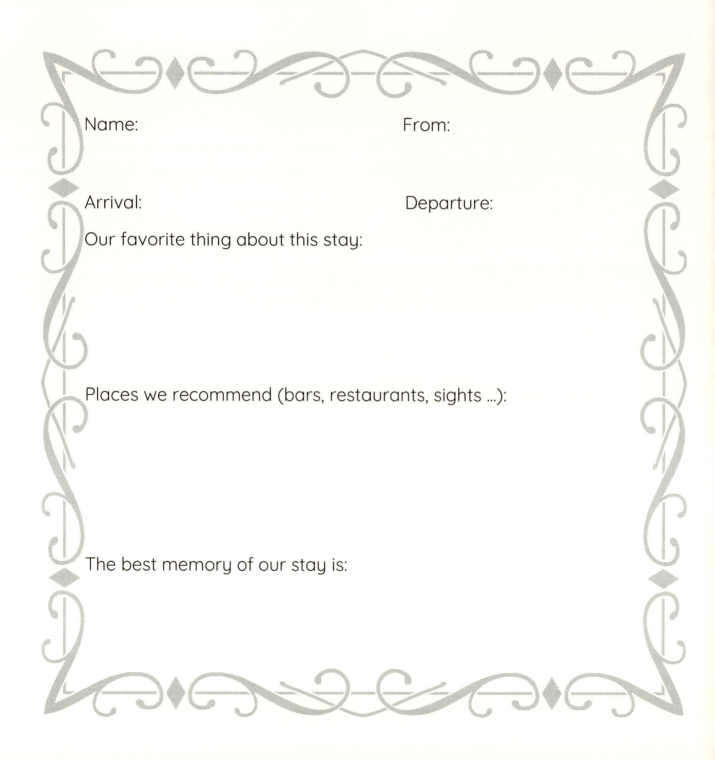

Name: From:

Arrival: Departure:

Our favorite thing about this stay:

Places we recommend (bars, restaurants, sights ...):

The best memory of our stay is:

Name: From:

Arrival: Departure:

Our favorite thing about this stay:

Places we recommend (bars, restaurants, sights ...):

The best memory of our stay is:

Name: From:

Arrival: Departure:

Our favorite thing about this stay:

Places we recommend (bars, restaurants, sights ...):

The best memory of our stay is:

Name: From:

Arrival: Departure:

Our favorite thing about this stay:

Places we recommend (bars, restaurants, sights ...):

The best memory of our stay is:

Name: From:

Arrival: Departure:

Our favorite thing about this stay:

Places we recommend (bars, restaurants, sights ...):

The best memory of our stay is:

Name: From:

Arrival: Departure:

Our favorite thing about this stay:

Places we recommend (bars, restaurants, sights ...):

The best memory of our stay is:

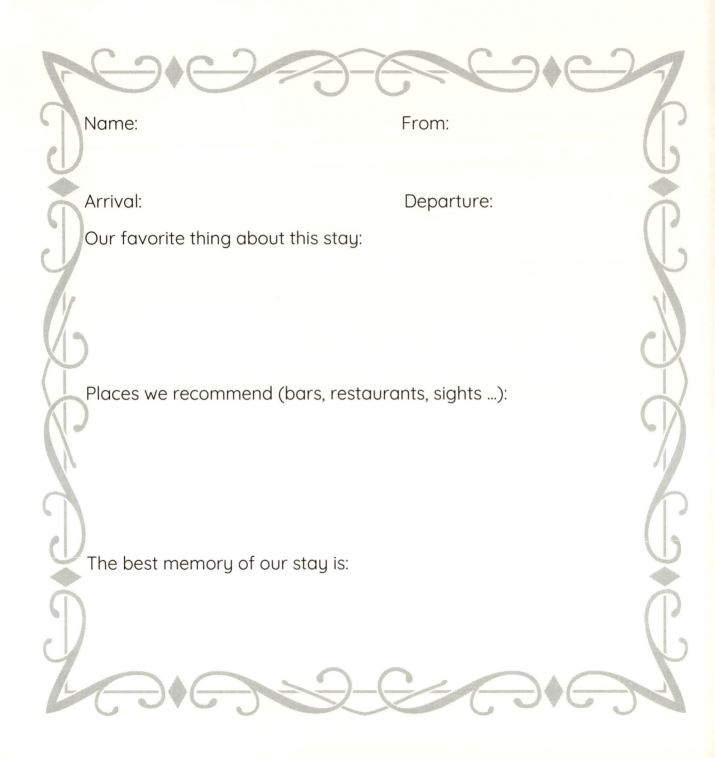

Name: From:

Arrival: Departure:

Our favorite thing about this stay:

Places we recommend (bars, restaurants, sights ...):

The best memory of our stay is:

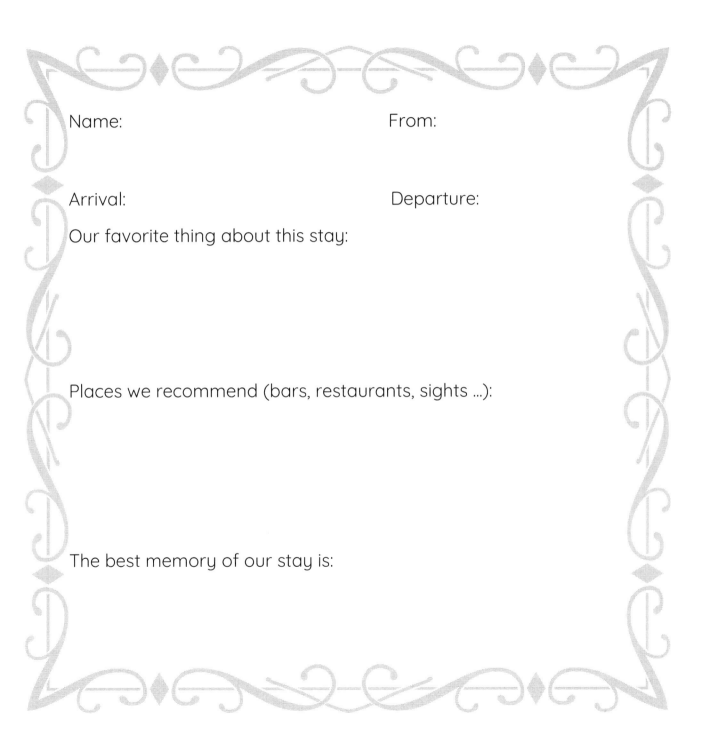

Name: From:

Arrival: Departure:

Our favorite thing about this stay:

Places we recommend (bars, restaurants, sights ...):

The best memory of our stay is:

Name: From:

Arrival: Departure:

Our favorite thing about this stay:

Places we recommend (bars, restaurants, sights ...):

The best memory of our stay is:

Name: From:

Arrival: Departure:

Our favorite thing about this stay:

Places we recommend (bars, restaurants, sights ...):

The best memory of our stay is:

Name: From:

Arrival: Departure:

Our favorite thing about this stay:

Places we recommend (bars, restaurants, sights ...):

The best memory of our stay is:

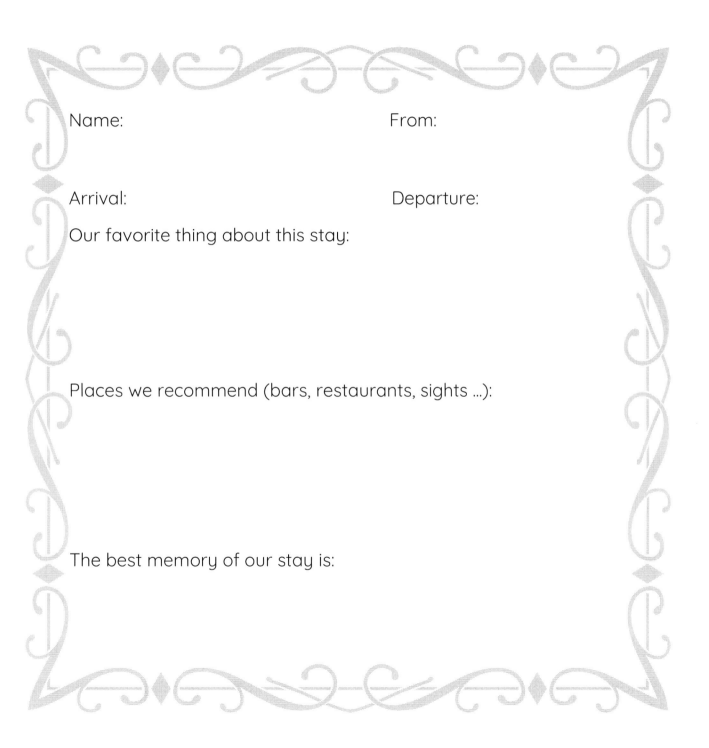

Name: From:

Arrival: Departure:

Our favorite thing about this stay:

Places we recommend (bars, restaurants, sights ...):

The best memory of our stay is:

Name: From:

Arrival: Departure:

Our favorite thing about this stay:

Places we recommend (bars, restaurants, sights ...):

The best memory of our stay is:

Name: From:

Arrival: Departure:

Our favorite thing about this stay:

Places we recommend (bars, restaurants, sights ...):

The best memory of our stay is:

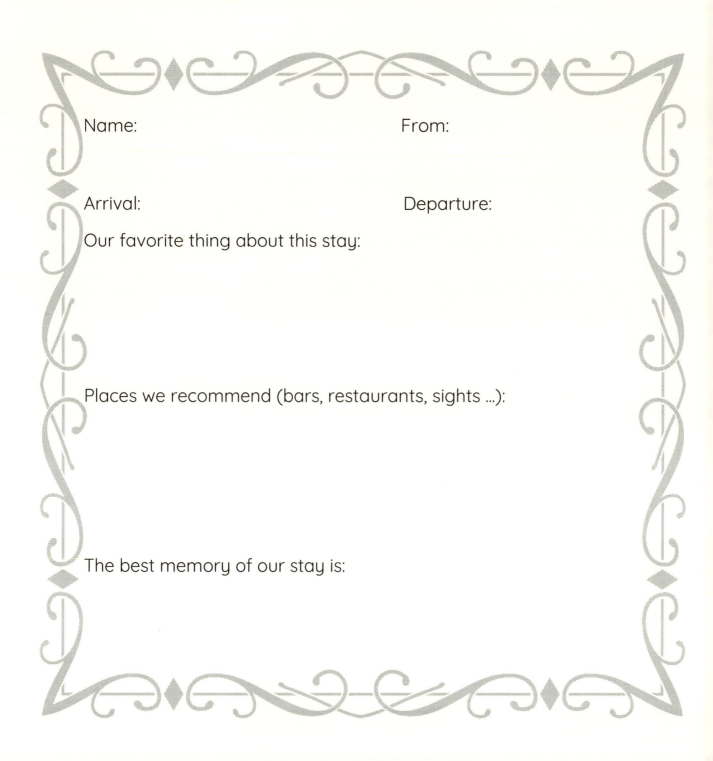

Name: From:

Arrival: Departure:

Our favorite thing about this stay:

Places we recommend (bars, restaurants, sights ...):

The best memory of our stay is:

Name: From:

Arrival: Departure:

Our favorite thing about this stay:

Places we recommend (bars, restaurants, sights ...):

The best memory of our stay is:

Name: From:

Arrival: Departure:

Our favorite thing about this stay:

Places we recommend (bars, restaurants, sights ...):

The best memory of our stay is:

Name: From:

Arrival: Departure:

Our favorite thing about this stay:

Places we recommend (bars, restaurants, sights ...):

The best memory of our stay is:

Name: From:

Arrival: Departure:

Our favorite thing about this stay:

Places we recommend (bars, restaurants, sights ...):

The best memory of our stay is:

Name: From:

Arrival: Departure:

Our favorite thing about this stay:

Places we recommend (bars, restaurants, sights ...):

The best memory of our stay is:

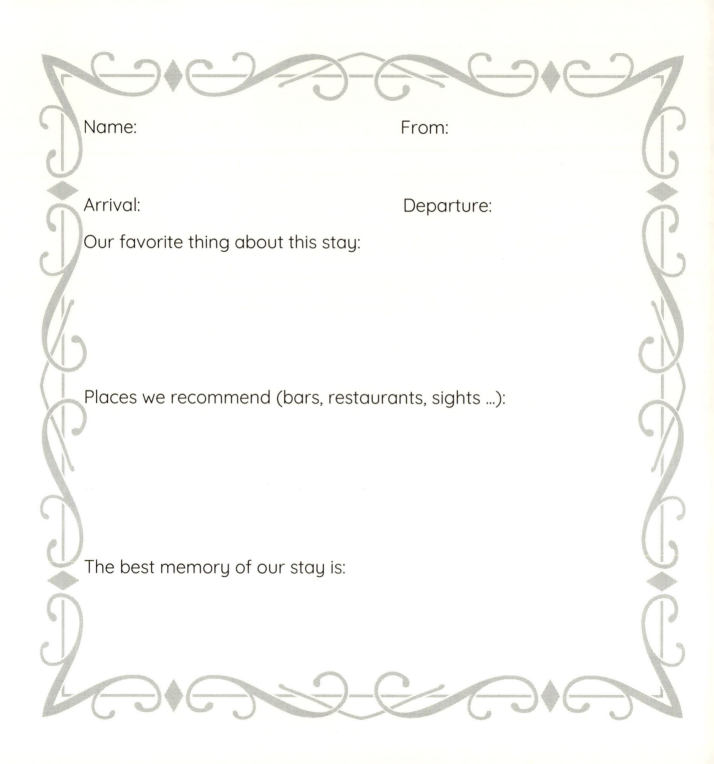

Name: From:

Arrival: Departure:

Our favorite thing about this stay:

Places we recommend (bars, restaurants, sights ...):

The best memory of our stay is:

Name: From:

Arrival: Departure:

Our favorite thing about this stay:

Places we recommend (bars, restaurants, sights ...):

The best memory of our stay is:

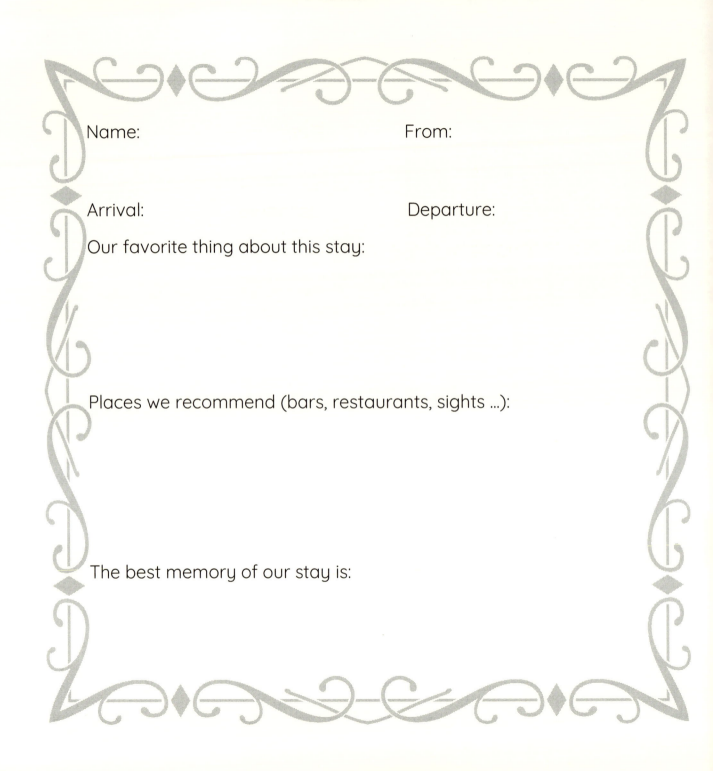

Name: From:

Arrival: Departure:

Our favorite thing about this stay:

Places we recommend (bars, restaurants, sights ...):

The best memory of our stay is:

Name: From:

Arrival: Departure:

Our favorite thing about this stay:

Places we recommend (bars, restaurants, sights ...):

The best memory of our stay is:

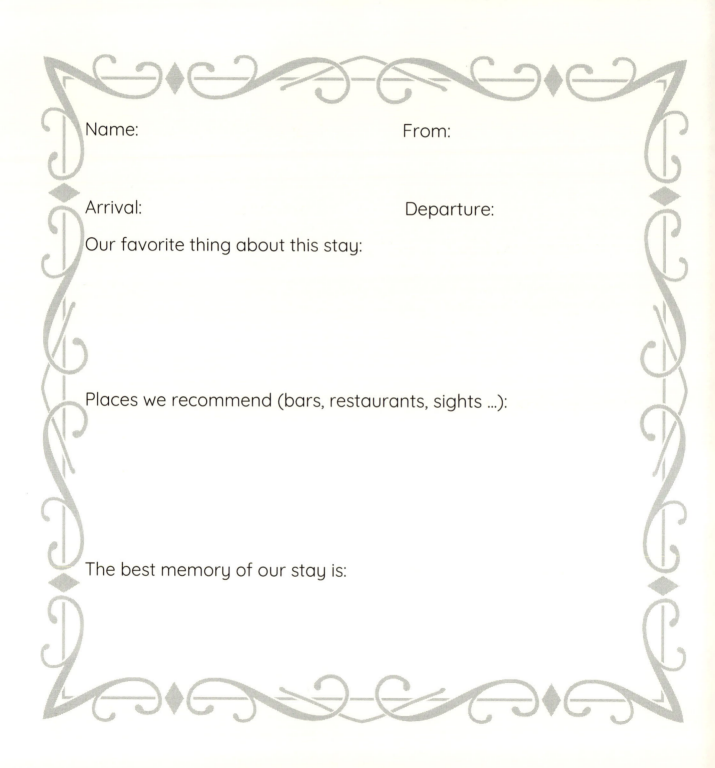

Name: From:

Arrival: Departure:

Our favorite thing about this stay:

Places we recommend (bars, restaurants, sights ...):

The best memory of our stay is:

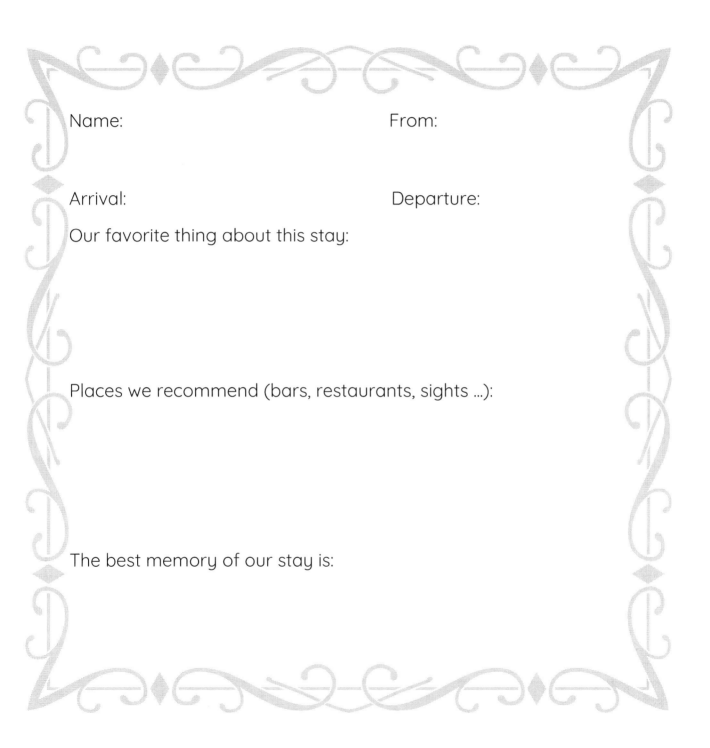

Name: From:

Arrival: Departure:

Our favorite thing about this stay:

Places we recommend (bars, restaurants, sights ...):

The best memory of our stay is:

Name: From:

Arrival: Departure:

Our favorite thing about this stay:

Places we recommend (bars, restaurants, sights ...):

The best memory of our stay is:

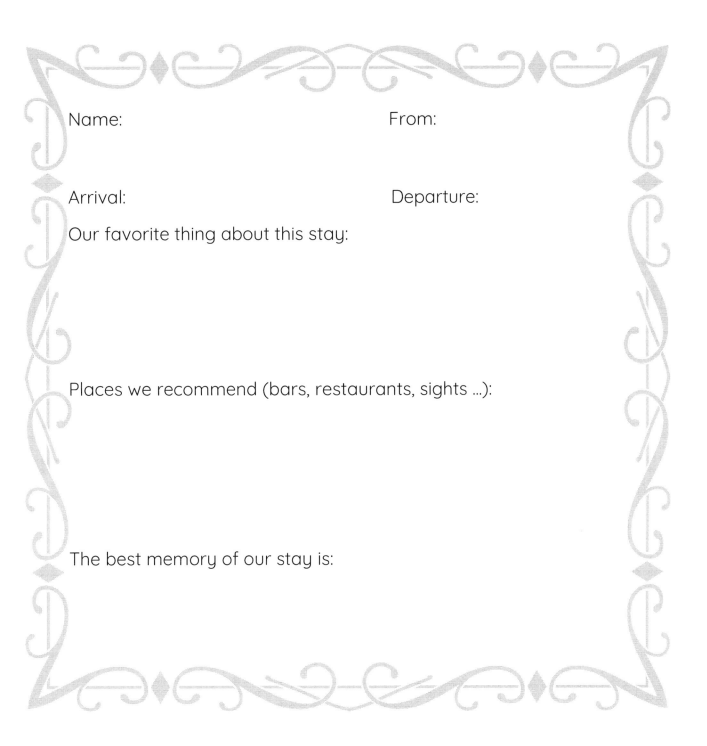

Name: From:

Arrival: Departure:

Our favorite thing about this stay:

Places we recommend (bars, restaurants, sights ...):

The best memory of our stay is:

Name: From:

Arrival: Departure:

Our favorite thing about this stay:

Places we recommend (bars, restaurants, sights ...):

The best memory of our stay is:

Name: From:

Arrival: Departure:

Our favorite thing about this stay:

Places we recommend (bars, restaurants, sights ...):

The best memory of our stay is:

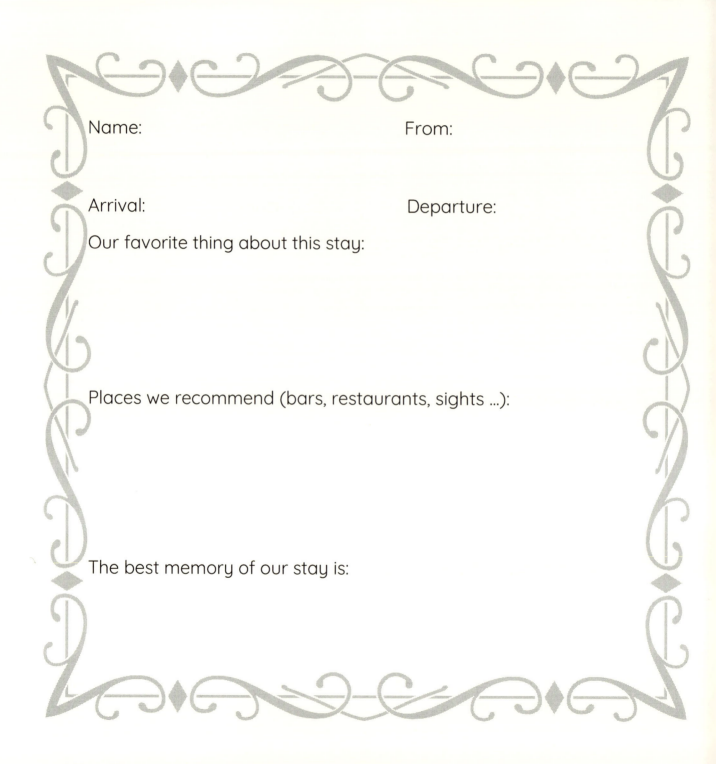

Name: From:

Arrival: Departure:

Our favorite thing about this stay:

Places we recommend (bars, restaurants, sights ...):

The best memory of our stay is:

Name: From:

Arrival: Departure:

Our favorite thing about this stay:

Places we recommend (bars, restaurants, sights ...):

The best memory of our stay is:

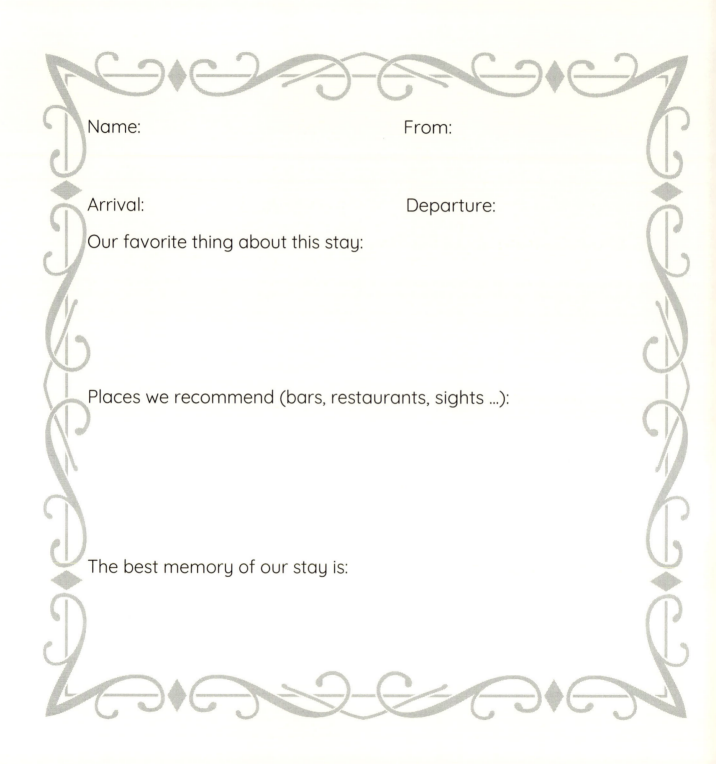

Name: From:

Arrival: Departure:

Our favorite thing about this stay:

Places we recommend (bars, restaurants, sights ...):

The best memory of our stay is:

Name: From:

Arrival: Departure:

Our favorite thing about this stay:

Places we recommend (bars, restaurants, sights ...):

The best memory of our stay is:

Name: From:

Arrival: Departure:

Our favorite thing about this stay:

Places we recommend (bars, restaurants, sights ...):

The best memory of our stay is:

Name: From:

Arrival: Departure:

Our favorite thing about this stay:

Places we recommend (bars, restaurants, sights ...):

The best memory of our stay is:

Name: From:

Arrival: Departure:

Our favorite thing about this stay:

Places we recommend (bars, restaurants, sights ...):

The best memory of our stay is:

Name: From:

Arrival: Departure:

Our favorite thing about this stay:

Places we recommend (bars, restaurants, sights ...):

The best memory of our stay is:

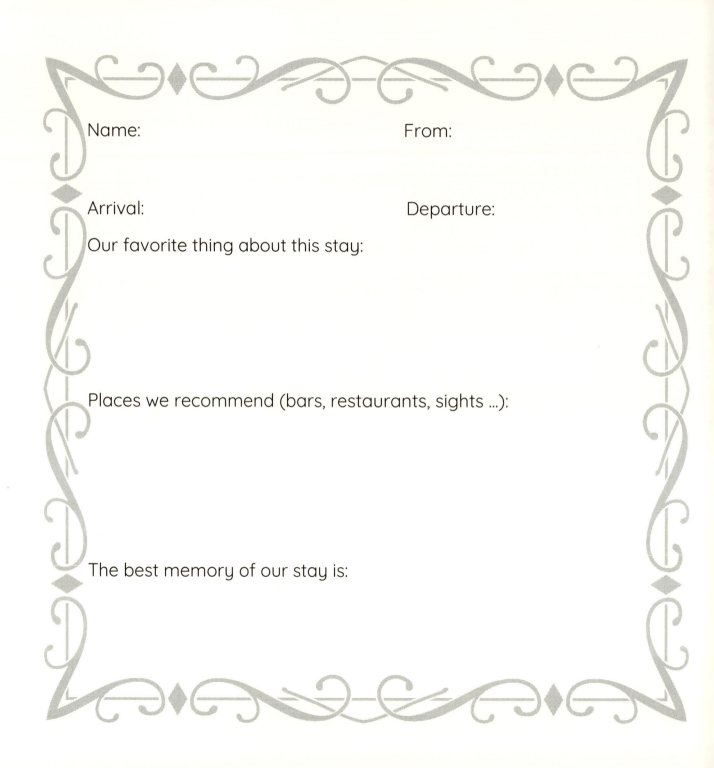

Name: From:

Arrival: Departure:

Our favorite thing about this stay:

Places we recommend (bars, restaurants, sights ...):

The best memory of our stay is:

Name: From:

Arrival: Departure:

Our favorite thing about this stay:

Places we recommend (bars, restaurants, sights ...):

The best memory of our stay is:

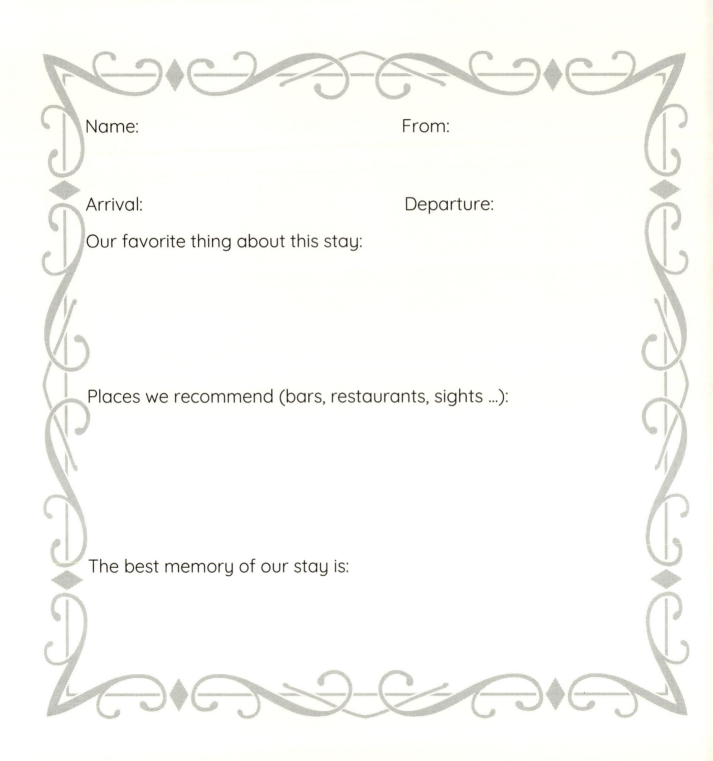

Name: From:

Arrival: Departure:

Our favorite thing about this stay:

Places we recommend (bars, restaurants, sights ...):

The best memory of our stay is:

Name: From:

Arrival: Departure:

Our favorite thing about this stay:

Places we recommend (bars, restaurants, sights ...):

The best memory of our stay is:

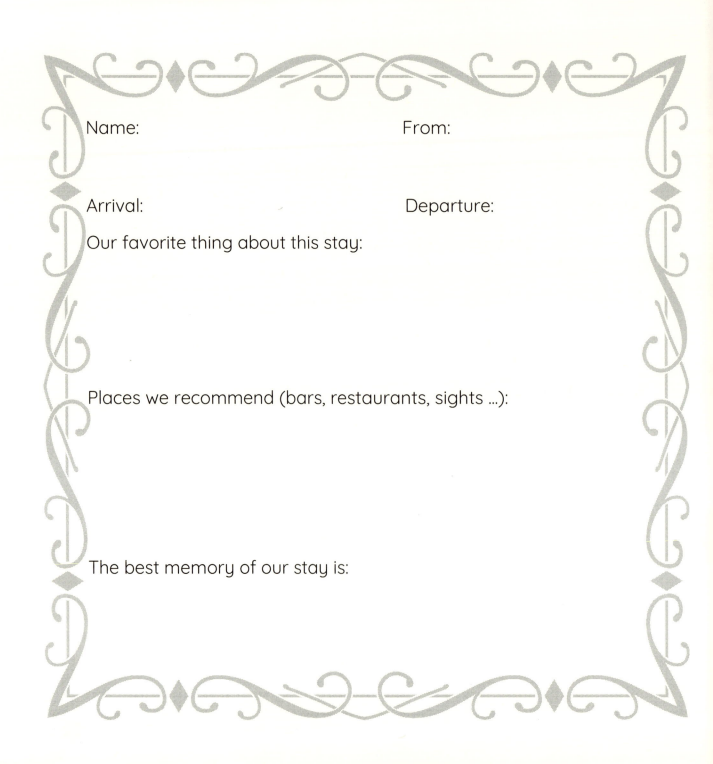

Name: From:

Arrival: Departure:

Our favorite thing about this stay:

Places we recommend (bars, restaurants, sights ...):

The best memory of our stay is:

Name: From:

Arrival: Departure:

Our favorite thing about this stay:

Places we recommend (bars, restaurants, sights ...):

The best memory of our stay is:

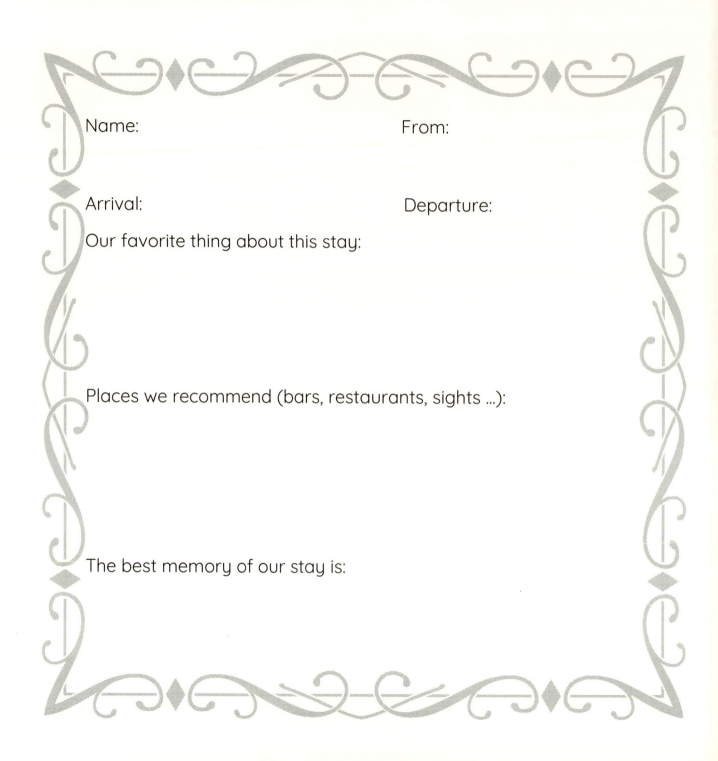

Name: From:

Arrival: Departure:

Our favorite thing about this stay:

Places we recommend (bars, restaurants, sights ...):

The best memory of our stay is:

Name: From:

Arrival: Departure:

Our favorite thing about this stay:

Places we recommend (bars, restaurants, sights ...):

The best memory of our stay is:

Name: From:

Arrival: Departure:

Our favorite thing about this stay:

Places we recommend (bars, restaurants, sights ...):

The best memory of our stay is:

Name: From:

Arrival: Departure:

Our favorite thing about this stay:

Places we recommend (bars, restaurants, sights ...):

The best memory of our stay is:

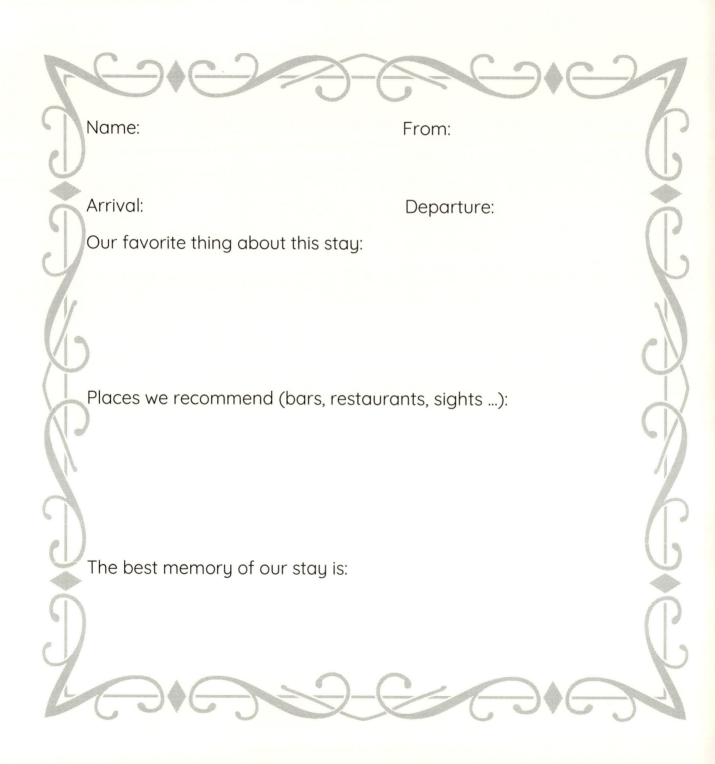

Name: From:

Arrival: Departure:

Our favorite thing about this stay:

Places we recommend (bars, restaurants, sights ...):

The best memory of our stay is:

Name: From:

Arrival: Departure:

Our favorite thing about this stay:

Places we recommend (bars, restaurants, sights ...):

The best memory of our stay is:

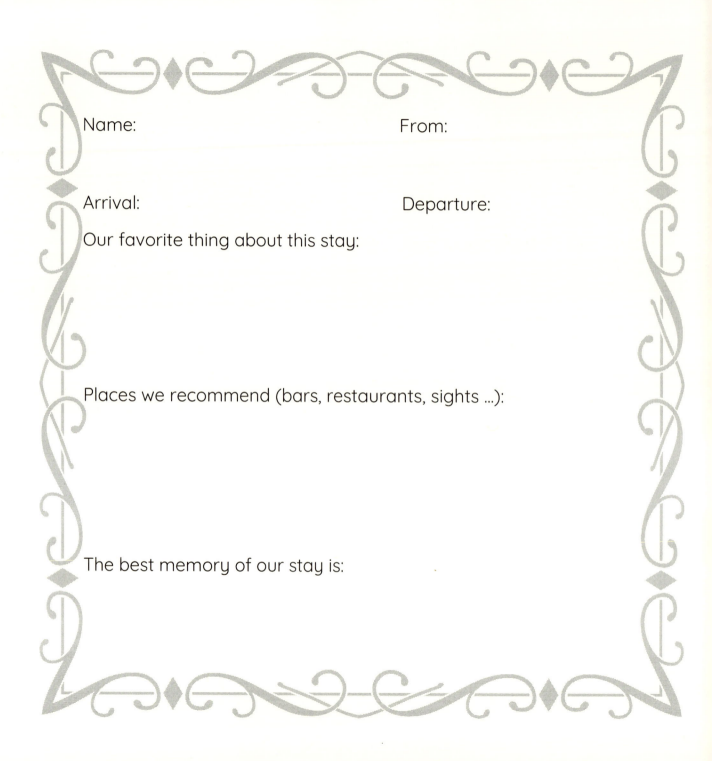

Name: From:

Arrival: Departure:

Our favorite thing about this stay:

Places we recommend (bars, restaurants, sights ...):

The best memory of our stay is:

Name: From:

Arrival: Departure:

Our favorite thing about this stay:

Places we recommend (bars, restaurants, sights ...):

The best memory of our stay is:

Name: From:

Arrival: Departure:

Our favorite thing about this stay:

Places we recommend (bars, restaurants, sights ...):

The best memory of our stay is:

Name: From:

Arrival: Departure:

Our favorite thing about this stay:

Places we recommend (bars, restaurants, sights ...):

The best memory of our stay is:

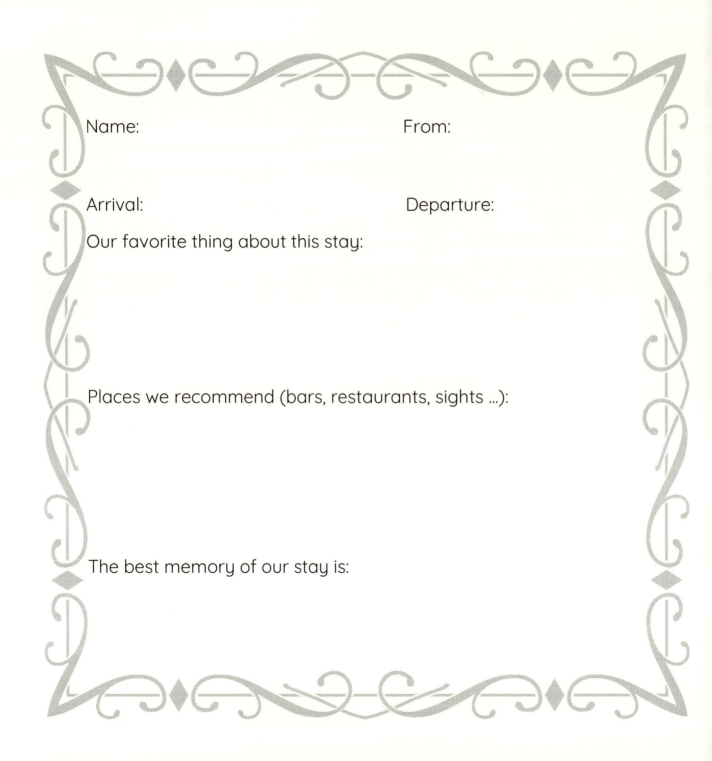

Name: From:

Arrival: Departure:

Our favorite thing about this stay:

Places we recommend (bars, restaurants, sights ...):

The best memory of our stay is:

Name: From:

Arrival: Departure:

Our favorite thing about this stay:

Places we recommend (bars, restaurants, sights ...):

The best memory of our stay is:

Name: From:

Arrival: Departure:

Our favorite thing about this stay:

Places we recommend (bars, restaurants, sights ...):

The best memory of our stay is:

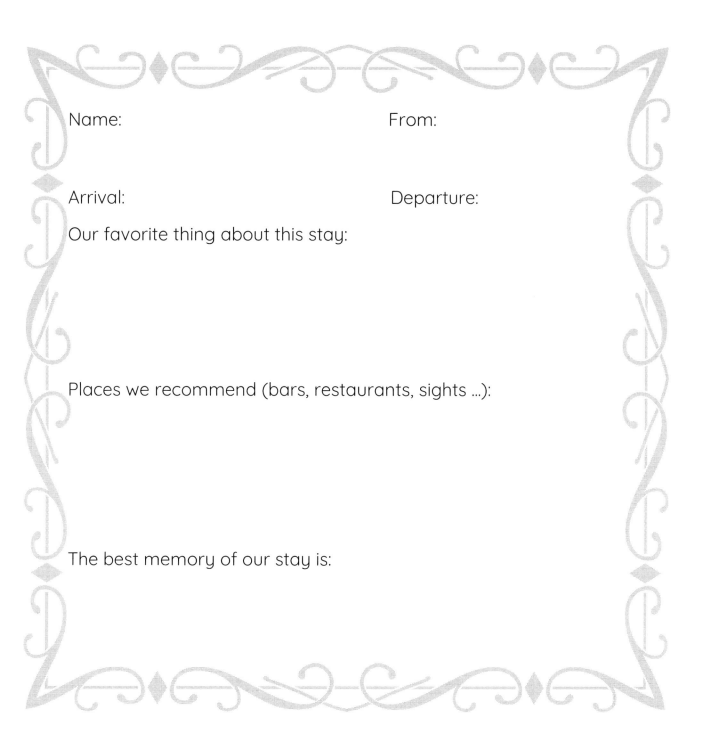

Name: From:

Arrival: Departure:

Our favorite thing about this stay:

Places we recommend (bars, restaurants, sights ...):

The best memory of our stay is:

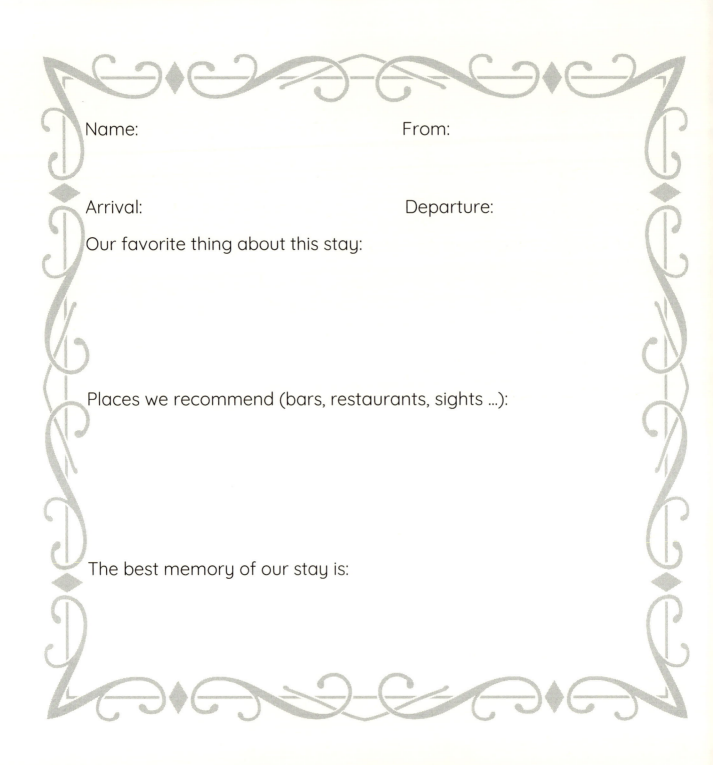

Name: From:

Arrival: Departure:

Our favorite thing about this stay:

Places we recommend (bars, restaurants, sights ...):

The best memory of our stay is:

Name: From:

Arrival: Departure:

Our favorite thing about this stay:

Places we recommend (bars, restaurants, sights ...):

The best memory of our stay is:

Name: From:

Arrival: Departure:

Our favorite thing about this stay:

Places we recommend (bars, restaurants, sights ...):

The best memory of our stay is:

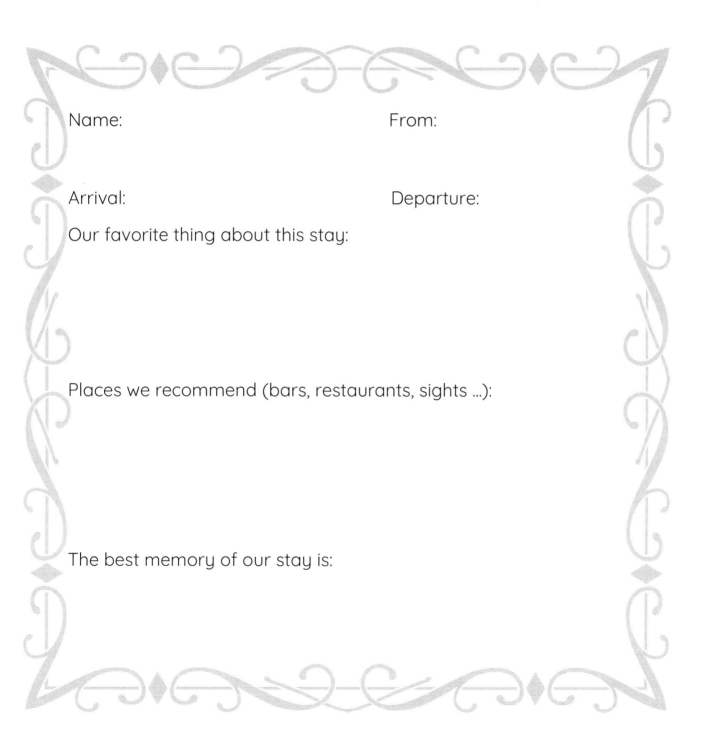

Name: From:

Arrival: Departure:

Our favorite thing about this stay:

Places we recommend (bars, restaurants, sights ...):

The best memory of our stay is:

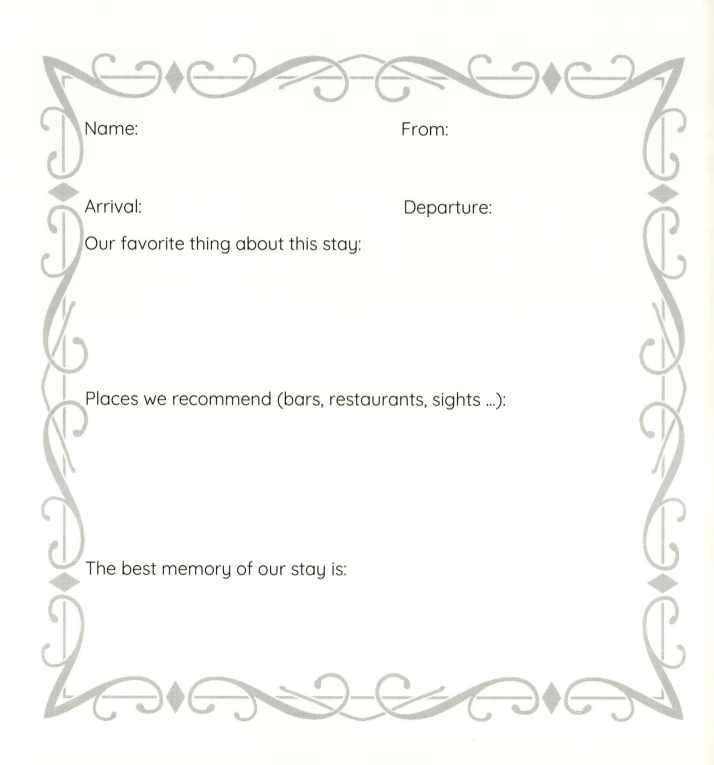

Name: From:

Arrival: Departure:

Our favorite thing about this stay:

Places we recommend (bars, restaurants, sights ...):

The best memory of our stay is:

Name: From:

Arrival: Departure:

Our favorite thing about this stay:

Places we recommend (bars, restaurants, sights ...):

The best memory of our stay is:

June 2019
© 2019 Stefan Waidelich Dachenhäuserweg 44.71101 Schönaich rockasteve@web.de
Druckerei: Amazon Media EU S.á r.l., 5 Rue Plaetis, L-2338, Luxembourg

Cover: © Canva Creative Commens Licence

Design: Pixa Heros Stuttgart

Made in United States
Orlando, FL
19 May 2022

17998016R00121